1987

BOOKS ON STAGECRAFT

Theory and Craft of the Scenographic Model
Darwin Reid Payne
A precise step-by-step guide to scenic model making
cloth 1193-3   paper 1194-1

Stage Rigging Handbook
Jay O. Glerum
A thorough guide to the safe use and care of stage rigging
comb binding 1318-9

Theatrical Scene Painting
A Lesson Guide
William Pinnell
All the proven techniques of traditional scene painting
paper 1332-4

Sceno-Graphic Techniques
W. Oren Parker
"The original text on theater drafting" in a new,
revised edition
paper 1350-2

Theatrical Scene Painting

A LESSON GUIDE

William H. Pinnell

Southern Illinois University Press • Carbondale and Edwardsville

To Jenny

Library of Congress Cataloging-in-Publication Data
Pinnell, William H.
Theatrical scene painting.
1. Scene painting—Technique. I. Title.
ND2885.P56 1987 750′.28 86-15500
ISBN 0-8093-1332-4 (pbk.)

The paper used in this publication meets the minimum
requirements of American National Standard for Information
Sciences – Permanence of Paper for Printed Library Materials,
ANSI Z39.48-1984. ∞™

Contents

Preface

All stage scenery strives for a textural quality, a surface smoothness or roughness that will provoke a particular, albeit subconscious, emotional reaction in the spectator. One does not react or relate equally to textures of coarse stucco, plush velvet, aged wood, or polished chrome. Through the setting, the scenic designer uses, among other tools, textures and dimensions to support the emotional qualities inherent in the play. Appropriate to the extent of the production budget, those textures may be three-dimensionally duplicated or achieved through the artistry of the scene painter.

The following work takes a very traditional and singular line. The techniques that form the foundation of traditional scene painting are what will be examined here, techniques employed to fool the eye into believing that two-dimensional surfaces possess a third dimension. Many devices and materials can be used to supplement the illusion of scene painting. Exciting and creative developments have been made with an aggregate of materials and textural aides. But this book is geared to the creative artist who, for lack of additional tools or for personal preference, must work with merely canvas and color.

Everything discussed and illustrated on the following pages is directed toward techniques employed in the realistic style of scene painting. But attempting to teach or learn and recognize realism is merely a starting point. Although realism and attempts to "mirror the real world" may be the foundation of one of the largest walls in the theatre, they do not necessarily provide the most enjoyable entertainment. Realism may, conversely, serve as a model from which we derive our own interpretations and create individual styles of expression.

Of course, scenery and its accompanying scene painting must blend into the style and interpretation of the production. And more often than not, a play will demand a realistic locale for the passage of its events. Accordingly, the painter must apply his knowledge of realistic impressions. But it is important that each and every painter in doing so not preoccupy him or herself with a quest for realistic duplication. Style must be encouraged. For with the development of style, self-assessments of aptitude and strong and weak points will occur. With the strong points will come the confidence needed to expand and experiment. With the weak points, ideally, efforts will be made to overcome shortcomings or find alternate approaches.

What will result will be the individual painter—a painter who, through experimentation, has developed a uniqueness of expression unlike any other painter. And, after all, is that not what the theatre is about: to develop an ability to perceive, evaluate, and create an expression that is distinctly individual, meaningful, and entertaining?

Scene painting can be pleasurable or a devastatingly arduous and tedious experience. The hours can be long and your wardrobe will take a good beating if you are not suitably dressed. The importance of preplanning and organization cannot be minimized. Preparation is the key. Carefully plot what has to be done and verify the sequence of painting steps that best suit your working habits. Make sure the scenery has been fully prepared for painting and is securely in position. Is there enough floor space for safe mobility? There is nothing worse than having to walk uphill no matter which direction you head. Have extra surfaces been set aside for testing paint samples? Finally, are there enough buckets, containers, and stir sticks available to mix your colors? The next morning you will thank yourself for quitting earlier the day before so the painting area could be cleaned and reorganized.

Most importantly, make every effort to keep your work enjoyable. Take a break when you need it. Don't push for the marathon sessions. Remember that your painting is making a valuable contribution to the production and is no less important and integral to its success than any other element. Your role is an expressive one, but unlike any other in the theatre, it can only be achieved by the sympathetic stroke of the painter's brush.

Acknowledgments

Special thanks for the generous assistance of Alvin Ade and the technical theatre staff at the University of Windsor. I also wish to gratefully acknowledge the support and patience of Kelly and my mother and father, without whose love, advice, and encouragement this book would never have been written.

Theatrical Scene Painting

Part 1. Materials and Techniques of Texture

Texture on stage scenery may be achieved in two ways: ACTUAL or SIMULATED. Actual textures take a three-dimensional form and may be constructed by using dimensional replicas or by building up the scenic surface with substitutes such as fiber glass, styrofoam, carpeting, plastics, etc. Simulated textures are achieved through the talents of scene painting in which the audience is fooled into believing that a surface is actually textured. Not only can the scene painter produce a wide variety of textures, but he can also create illusions of depth and distance.

The scene painter employs a number of tools to achieve texture: varying shapes and sizes of brushes, as well as sponges, fabric, sprayers, rollers, feather dusters, and string. One need only look around, for there is really no limit to what can be used. The utensils covered in this book are time-tested; they may, however, be abandoned or substituted according to the preference or style of the individual painter.

But before further discussions on texture through scene painting, it is necessary to outline the working requirements of space and materials one will need before this art of illusion can begin.

1. Space

A good working area is essential. Many professional scene shops and theatres have large wooden PAINT FRAMES, hung vertically, to which

1

drops, scrims and other forms of two-dimensional scenery may be attached. The frame is permanently attached to the back wall of the theatre or paint shop, or it may be of such a nature that it can be raised or lowered through a slit in the floor, allowing the scenic artist to remain on one level without climbing ladders (fig. 1).

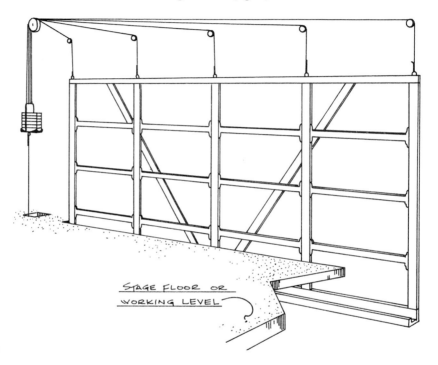

STAGE FLOOR OR
WORKING LEVEL

Figure 1

If the paint frame is stationary, the scene painter may either work on a movable bridge or use a BOOMERANG. A boomerang is a construction on casters much resembling a flight of steps with convenient landings so the scene painter can change his elevation and paint the scenery before him with ease (fig. 2).

Should a paint frame not be available and large drops or scrims have to be painted, a room with adequate floor space is necessary. Individual flats can be painted on their sides or, if ceiling space allows, may be stood upright. Should the room's available height be a restriction, the scenery must be placed flat on the floor. The method of painting scenery while it is lying face up on the floor is called the CONTINENTAL SYSTEM. Actually, many scene painters prefer the continental method for paint-

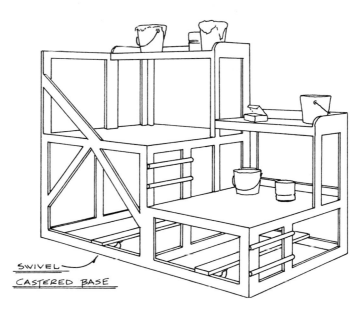

Figure 2

ing most of their scenery, regardless of the space and facilities available. They contend the control of both paint and brush are more secure than upright painting where gravity is the enemy and may cause the unwanted and frustrating dripping of paint. The adjustment from the vertical to the horizontal method of painting is a relatively simple one, but does require practice. Brushes are often attached to boards and bamboo sticks to save on the possible back strain of the painter. Not only can the painter work with ease, but the paint is, through gravity, always running from the ferrule to the point of the brush thereby lessening the number of times it must be recharged. An additional advantage to the continental method rests in the retarded drying time of the paints and dyes. Because air cannot readily circulate between the scenery and the floor, paints will remain wetter longer and allow additional time for the wet mixing of colors if desired.

When continentally painting flats, the floor should be covered with brown Kraft paper to catch spilled or refuse paint. When painting drops or scrims on the floor, gray bogus paper as an undercovering should be used to allow evenness in drying. (Make sure the *rough* side of the bogus paper is facing up to allow maximum absorption.) Kraft paper, on the other hand, should not be used under drops and scrims, as it does not absorb water well and will buckle when wet. Commercially available waxed paper should be used when gluing appliques or reinforcing cut drops with scrim or scenic netting. The waxed paper will peel away from the rear of the drops and scrims, whereas gray bogus paper will stick.

A warm, dry atmosphere is a distinct asset. The consistencies of most paints and dyes react unfavorably to cold, and the drying time will be markedly and inconveniently retarded.

2. Equipment

Buckets and Containers

Even for painting small, simple pieces of scenery, buckets and tins in which to mix paint are needed. It is wise to have a few 5-gallon containers available should large quantities of paint be required. Eight to ten plastic buckets (2–3 gal. capacity) with shaped pour spouts are a must. Several tin cans, commercially referred to as no. 10 size, will prove very handy for smaller quantities of special colors (fig. 3 [dozens of these cans are thrown out daily by restaurants and cafeterias]).

An asset for the painter who must move from area to area in the shop is the paint carrier (fig. 4). This handy device not only provides for the easy mobility of colors but helps prevent the spilling of paint and includes a storage area for extra brushes, charcoal sticks, and felt tip

Figure 3   <u>5 GALLON</u>   <u>2–3 GAL.</u>   <u>No. 10</u>

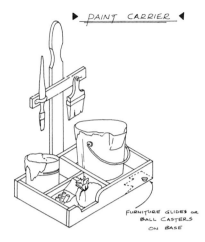

PAINT CARRIER

FURNITURE GLIDES OR
BALL CASTERS
ON BASE

Figure 4

markers. On its base are metal furniture glides, which minimize the possibility of damage to the horizontal painting surface when the carrier is moved.

Brushes

The brush is the painter's most prized possession. To the sensitive painter, each brush in his collection has its own unique feel and special purpose. The more superstitious of painters will only work with their own brushes and claim that borrowed brushes are unsuitable, inferior, and simply will not work for them. Regardless of individual habits, preferences, and eccentricities, every painter is aware that no one brush will serve all painting needs and that a repertoire of shapes and sizes are required to fulfill painting and stroke requirements.

The diagram in figure 5 illustrates the components of the paint brush. The shape of the bristle and ferrule and the length and shape of the handle determine the type of brush and its recommended usage.

The brushes common to scene painting are displayed in fig. 6:

1. A large brush called a PRIMER, 5–6 inches in width, would be advantageous. Its bristles are soft and should not be confused with a whitewashing brush. As its name would suggest, it is used to treat newly covered flats with a sealing coat of paint. The larger the brush the more smoothly and quickly large areas can be covered. The primer brush may also be used for applying base coats of paint. Order through a theatrical supplier.

5

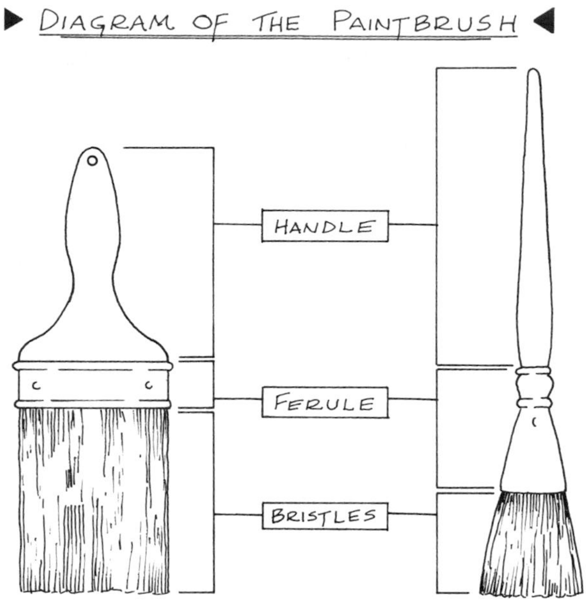

▶ DIAGRAM OF THE PAINTBRUSH ◀

HANDLE

FERULE

BRISTLES

Figure 5

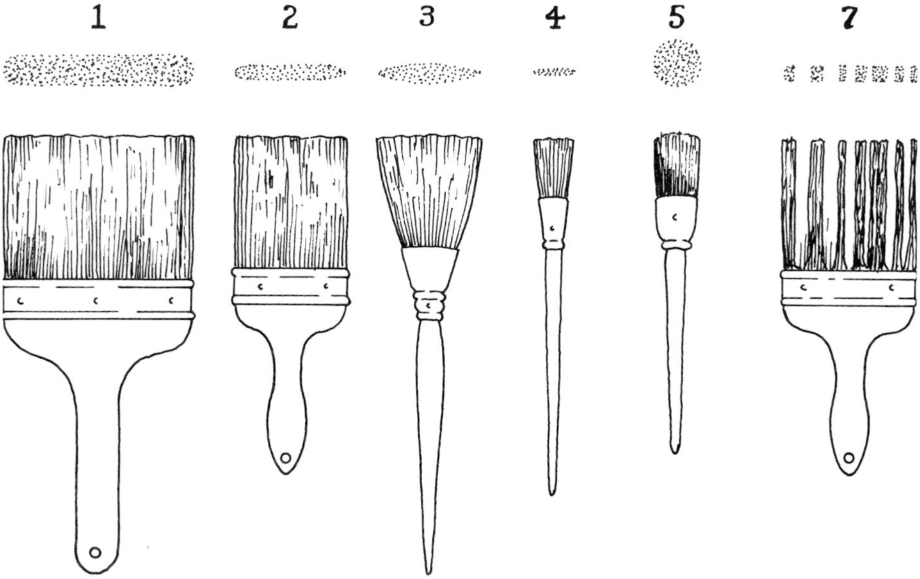

1　　2　　3　　4　　5　　7

Figure 6

2. LAY-IN brushes come in 3-inch, 4-inch, and 5-inch widths. They cover rapidly and cut sharp edges when twisted. Brushes of this nature can be purchased in any paint or hardware store, but be sure to choose ones with relatively soft bristles. (Those referred to as "latex brushes" will work well.) Bristle length is also important. The longer the bristle, the more paint the brush will hold.

3. FOLIAGE BRUSHES, sometimes called FANTAILS, range from 1 1/2 to 3 1/2 inches in width at the ferrule. Their unique bristle shape allows for graceful imprints when the edge of the bristle's length is pressed against the painting surface. Like the primer brush, fantails are purchased through theatrical painting and supply houses.

4. Small, long-handled brushes are called LINER BRUSHES (or FITCHES) and will range from a 1/4-inch cutting brush to 1 1/2 inches in width. These brushes possess a sharp chisel point and are used primarily for detail work and touch-ups and are available through theatrical suppliers.

Other brushes employed are:

5. STENCIL BRUSHES have a round ferrule and are used to pound paint through stencils. Theatrical suppliers.

6. PUSH BRUSHES or BROOMS are ordinary long-handled janitor's brooms with softened bristles for continental painting techniques. Hardware and home centers.

7. SPECIALTY BRUSHES are those adapted by invention or from older or worn brushes. One common example is the CUT BRISTLE BRUSH that is used for graining, cloth-fiber appearances, and general linear texturing. Clumps of bristles have either fallen out or been removed.

If one is serious about scene painting, it is worthwhile to buy best-quality brushes. Brushes resembling those described above might often be found at hardware and paint stores. But for scene-painting needs, it is best to shop through a theatrical supplier where one can be sure the brushes purchased suit theatrical needs. European white bristle liner and fantail brushes are extremely durable if properly used, cleaned, and stored. Artist easel brushes may find a calling for special painting needs but are generally of too hard or soft a bristle texture for scene painting needs.

Paint and Dye

There are many types of paints and dyes used in painting scenery. The most commonly employed, though not in order of preference, are

1. dry pigments
2. casein
3. vinyl paint
4. latex
5. aniline dye
6. bronze powders

Of the above, there are many derivatives available and the combined usage of several on one painting project is not uncommon. For purity and clarity, each is described below for its singular characteristics and individual usage.

1. DRY PIGMENTS are the oldest and most "traditional" form of scene paint. Purchased by the pound and in powder form, dry pigments must be mixed with a binder, or glue solution. If mixed only with water, the paint will dry back to its original powdered state and not adhere to the scenery. Though almost any type of binder may be used with this kind of scene paint, the one type that will not dull the vibrancy of the powder pigments and is certainly the most economical in the long run is called SIZE WATER. Ground or flake gelatin glue and water are the ingredients of traditional size water (see below). When dry, however, powder pigments lack the permanence of casein, vinyl, or latex and may need to be "sealed," or covered, by a waterproof glaze (i.e., latex and vinyl) to prevent the pigments from rubbing off. WHITING is used to stretch the quantity of the paint and then tinted to the appropriate color with other more expensive and exotic dry pigment colors. On the cheaper end of the price scale is the whiting, while the price of pigments per pound increases as the colors become more brilliant. It is important to note that dry pigments are at least 3 times darker when wet. Therefore, many painters will mix their colors first in powder form, thus approximating the value of the paint after it has dried, and then add the binder and mix to the desired consistency.

2. CASEIN, along with vinyl colors, is a very popular medium because of its ease in workability. Casein contains its own binder and contains a derivative of a compound found in milk. It can be poured from the can in its thin paste form and conveniently mixed with warm water. Dyes may be added to casein to deepen and strengthen its tone. Completely waterproof when dry, casein can be washed when soiled with a light solution of soap and water. Offering good hiding power, it may also be thinned to a wash and will mix readily with other water-based media. Because of its durability, casein may be covered with glazes of dyes or

thinned paints without being rubbed up. Its flat drying finish is slightly lighter when dry. Shelf life is excellent if tightly sealed, while adding a small amount of water to the top of the paint to keep it moist.

3. VINYL PAINTS come in liquid form, contain their own binder, and are thinned with water. Like casein and latex colors, its principal attributes lie in the convenience of preparation and workability, in addition to permanence. It does, however, lack the brilliance of dry pigment colors and is not as vivid as casein, but it can be heightened (or enriched) by adding aniline dye or casein paint. Vinyl paint is available in flat or semigloss, and applied straight from the can is very durable for painting floors and platforms. Thinned to a normal paint consistency, it can be used on muslin or canvas, while further thinning will produce an excellent glaze. While clear liquid vinyls can be used to waterproof dry pigment colors, clear GLOSS vinyl will add an extra dimension of richness to wood graining, a luster to marblized units, etc.

4. LATEX PAINTS have become available in wide ranges of colors but have a tendency to gray very slightly when dry. Alkyd-latex (its formal name) comes in paste form and has a base containing synthetic rubber. Readily thinned with water, latex dries to permanency. Latex contains its own binder and can be scrubbed clean when applied to material or wood. It will form its own resilient surface that will accept glazes of casein, vinyl, or aniline dye. Latex will not adhere well to nonporous surfaces, such as plastic or glass, unless thinned to a glaze; thicker or paste consistencies will shortly peel away. Latex is available in flat, semigloss, and clear varities. Clear latex, which somewhat resembles heavy cream when wet, dries completely transparent and with a gloss. The degree of glossiness is controlled by the amount of water used to thin the mixture. Working straight from the can will result in a highly polished look. Thinned with water, or diluted with a latex wash, clear latex is excellent for increasing surface richness and as a "fixative" for dry pigments. As with clear liquid vinyls, expect a darkening of the painted surface, particuarly when setting dry pigments.

5. ANILINE DYES come in both powder and crystal forms and most are soluble in hot water, while some are alcohol soluble. (Even those dyes that claim to be water soluble may need a dram of alcohol to break down any resistance). CAUTION: *Aniline dyes contain an extract of benzene, a poisonous liquid obtained from coal tar. Work in a well-ventilated area and take frequent breaks.* As the name suggests, a "dye" is a permanent medium. It can be used to bleed or puddle on fabric backdrops, enhance the beauty of a velour's texture, pull out the grain of raw wood,

9

create a dreamlike mist on a scrim, or cast superb shadow-wash glazes. Dyes must be used and prepared with care. The general rule is to prepare a dye that is a little weak, rather than one that is too strong. The darker you want the effect, the more applications of dye should be used. Dye only works one way: it DARKENS. To lighten is to bleach. Dye that has been mixed too strongly will often crystallize and virtually change its own color. To be safe, and to assure permanence, aniline dyes can be made extrapermanent by mixing them with binders of size water, white glue, or clear vinyl. Ordering is by the pound.

6. BRONZE POWDERS are available in a wide range of colors. These metallic pigments are expensive but, in terms of traditional scene painting, are indispensable. They are perfect for gilding architectural ornaments, picture frames, set and hand props; highlighting decorative filigree and drapery tassels; or stenciling on drops and flats. Metallic powders can be used on wood, plastic, metal, or fabric. Frugally added to paint, bronzes will float to the surface of the painting as it dries to lend a metallic glaze. Though bronze powders can be mixed with many types of binders, virtually all forms will dull the metallic pigment to certain degrees. For minimal discoloration, mix with clear gloss vinyl (2 parts vinyl to 1 part water).

Dry Pigments

With all of the above types of durable and convenient paints available, it seems surprising that dry pigment is still a medium in common use. But far cheaper in bulk quantities than any of the others, this traditional paint also offers perhaps the most brilliant intensities of theatrical paint colors available. Its main drawbacks are in its time-consuming processes of preparation and preserving. Relying on a separate binder as its liquifying agent, SIZE WATER (ground or flake glue + water) is the most common. Though many other binder solutions are available, this least expensive binder is made with flake or ground GELATIN glue. Sometimes referred to as "animal glue" because of the origin of its primary components, this sturdy gelatin glue has been used for centuries without parallel as an agent for carpenters, sailors, and theatre craftsmen.

To prepare the glue. Fill a 1-gallon metal bucket 3/4 full and cover the glue with cold water until the water is approximately 1 inch above the level of the glue. Let stand overnight. This will allow the glue particles to partially dissolve and expand. The next morning heat this bucket in an-

10

other bucket (a large double boiler arrangement) partially filled with water to prevent it from burning. Should the glue be allowed to burn or smoke because the water has evaporated, one will get an immediate understanding and appreciation of the apt labeling "animal glue." (As an alternative to the ground or flake form, premixed slabs of glue can be purchased from theatrical suppliers. Chunks are cut off, heated, and liquefied to the desired consistency. Available as well are electric glue pots that have temperature controls and will eliminate much inconvenience.) After the water boils, and while stirring frequently, the glue will slowly turn to a heavy molasses consistency. This is called "strong size." If allowed to cool, this mixture will congeal to an extremely rubbery mass. Reheat for workability.

To make the working size, or the SIZE WATER that will be used to liquefy the dry pigments. Mix 10 parts hot water to 1 part strong size. This ratio is not sacred and will vary according to the manufacturer, so it is always best to set aside a sample surface for painting. Choose a surface identical to the actual painting surface. For instance, do not paint a test swatch on a piece of plywood if you are going to be painting on muslin or canvas. Paint has a tendency to soak further into wood than it does fabric and may create the false impression that the size water ratio is adequate. Accordingly, do not choose an old flat that has been painted many times. Several previous layers of dry pigment paint will eventually peel or crack. Painting over such a surface with a test swatch will give the false impression of an overly strong size water mixture.

When the painting sample dries, if it rubs off onto the fingers, the size water is too weak. If the surface cracks or peels, the size water is too strong.

3. Basic Color Mixing

For the beginning painter, the mixing of the paint sometimes takes longer than the actual scene painting. It is worthwhile to go to the precautions necessary to ensure the colors and consistencies are exactly right before the paint is applied to the scenery. The scene painter must have a thorough understanding of the harmony, balance, and sequence of colors as they vary in value and intensity. The mixing of colors is a fascinating task. If the scenic designer and scene painter are not the same person, then the role of the painter is one of duplicator of colors. The designer must provide the painter with a color rendering of the set, as most renderings attempt to capture the setting under stage-lighting conditions, in addition to a painter's elevation or swatches of color which have been pretested under lighting conditions.

The first step facing the painter is to identify the position that each of the color swatches occupies on the COLOR WHEEL. The color wheel is the most familiar graphic arrangement of color relationships used. The circular sequence shows the step-to-step formation of colors that eventually end at the point where the flow began. Observe the color wheel in figure 7. Within the circle is a six-pointed dotted figure, overlapped by a striped triangle that in turn is overlapped by a solid triangle.

The solid triangle points to three colors: yellow, red, and blue. These are called PRIMARIES because they cannot be mixed from other colors. Their pigments must be obtained from natural elements or plants containing those colors. The striped triangle points to the three colors cre-

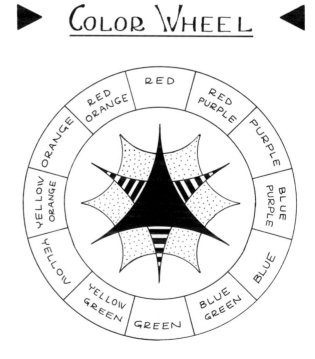

Figure 7

12

ated by the mixing of two equal quantities of primaries. The resulting orange, purple, and green are called the SECONDARIES. Actually, all colors other than the three primaries are secondary colors. The initial secondaries of green, purple, and orange are said to be the principal or central secondaries because of the equal ratio of their primary components. Lastly, the dotted figure points to six additional secondaries that are the results of the proportions of the two primary colors that are mixed to create them.

This color wheel, then, contains the twelve principal hues that make up the scene painter's palette. One might recognize colors similar to those on the wheel in the average paint store. No doubt the yellow green will not be called as such because the name is unexciting, albeit true to is base formula. Instead it might be labeled autumn avocado, for example, to increase its appeal. The very complex nomenclature of color is a problem in and of itself, even when ordering from theatrical suppliers, because there is a great discrepancy in the way the terms are used. Unfortunately individual terminology and definition are subject to particular tastes, preferences, and convenience.

As an example one company may offer a primary red pigment, while another company counters with the supposed equivalent spectrum red. By definition, a primary is an original hue in the light spectrum of color. Do not be surprised if the corresponding reds are very different in value. One may be a bluish red. That is, a red with blue cast, while the other may have touches of yellow as an additive. Anytime the primary is not a TRUE primary (and that is most of the time), the color is said to have CONTAMINATION.

Commercial colors usually have some degree of color contamination. Most have additives of white or black. The problem is that contamination is not uniform. If one were to be able to count on a certain degree of white contamination, say, in all of his colors he would be able to account for the contaminations in his mixing. However, the degree and colors of contaminants vary largely from color to color and company to company. One must be on guard for such variances and through experience learn to counteract their effect.

If one were to procure absolute primaries, equal quantities of the three mixed together would create black. Most commercial colors claiming to be primary or spectrum colors when mixed equally will produce either a deep gray or deep brown, depending on the contaminants used, instead of black. Any pairs of colors when mixed to produce black are called COMPLEMENTARIES. An easy way to discover a complement to a color is to match it with the color directly across from itself on the color wheel. For example, green is the complementary color of red. Mixing these together will create black ONLY IF COMBINED IN EQUAL PROPORTIONS. That is:

COMBINING:
1 quart of RED   with   2 quarts of GREEN
(1 qt. YELLOW + 1 qt. BLUE)
IS THE SAME AS AN EQUAL MIXTURE
OF THE THREE PRIMARIES
▶ Equals: BLACK ◀

Suppose we add 1 quart of red to 1 quart of green. In this case, break the colors down into smaller quantities. The red accounts for 2 pints of color. The true or central green is made of 1 pint each of yellow and blue. The 2 pints of yellow and blue combine with 1 pint of red to produce black (3 pts.). Left over will be 1 pint of red. The total result of the mixing will be a very dark red. Changing the ratios of any of the contributors will alter the value of the eventual hue.

Black was used in the past example to illustrate two points: 1) absolute primaries combined in equal proportion, or any true complementary colors combined in equal proportion, will produce black; and 2) black is integral in the mixing of colors when variation in color value is needed. The absence of black in the scheme of color mixing would be a monumental detriment.

Why, then, is black not included on the color wheel? It certainly does not fall into the category of a primary because it can be mixed from other colors. However, white cannot be found on the color wheel, yet it is like the primaries in that it cannot be mixed from other colors. Some proponents of color theory refer to black as the combination of all colors, and white as the absence of color. What is important to note is that black and white are used for tinting and shading purposes perhaps as frequently as those colors exhibited on the color wheel. Convenience would seem to dictate that one refer to them using the same term: color. In the practical mixing of color, primaries are used far less than the more complex colors, but being aware of the effects of primary and complementary combinations the experienced painter can cut many a corner and save quantities of paint by using amounts of black and/or white in appropriate measures.

Using Black and White

Any color can be described in three ways: its placement on the color wheel and the amounts of white or black it contains. Whites can be combined with any color and what will result is a TINT of the original color. Black added to color will create a SHADE. White and black admixtures greatly affect a total mixture of color, particularly when the amounts of black or white are large in quantity. A tremendously large number of tints and shades of any one color are possible to produce.

Mixed by themselves, black and white may be mixed in an infinite number of proportions. What has become standard for scene-painting needs is the Table of Nine Mixtures according to the following formula:

TABLE OF NINE MIXTURES
(Number refers to constant unit of
measure, e.g., 1 cup)

white 0
black 8

white 1
black 7

white 2
black 6

white 3
black 5

white 4
black 4

white 5
black 3

white 6
black 2

white 7
black 1

white 8
black 0

This column is a scale of mixture from black to white. The top combination represents a pure black and the bottom a pure white; those in between represent varying values of gray.

Begin to imagine, for example, the virtually limitless confines of color if one were to mix the medium (4 to 4) gray with purple. Beginning an entirely new scale similar to the black/white above, mix 8 parts purple with 0 parts medium gray and continue through to the end of the table, 0 to 8. If this series were continued with all values of gray from the above initial table, the result would be 49 different values of purple, excluding the pure purple and original values of gray resulting from 0 to 8, and 0 to 8, ratios. (Values of gray can be used to neutralize bright colors and lessen their vibrancy. The procedure is called "graying down" a color.)

The use of white alone with purple in the nine-mixture table will produce seven different tints of purple. Substituting black for the white will create seven shades. Because many of the black pigments available are contaminated, shades may appear to muddy the color. Always attempt, above any color, to purchase the purist of blacks and the most brilliant of whites available.

Scene-painting Palette (Dry Pigments)

When preparing a palette of colors one should use the TWELVE PRINCIPAL HUES as a guideline and attempt to select colors closest to the hues on the color wheel. These colors constitute a respectable, basic palette:

> yellow: LIGHT CHROME YELLOW
> yellow orange: MEDIUM CHROME YELLOW
> orange: AMERICAN VERMILION
> red: TURKEY RED LAKE
> red purple: MAGENTA LAKE
> purple: ROYAL PURPLE BLUE
> purple: VIOLET LAKE
> blue: COBALT BLUE
> blue green: CELESTIAL BLUE
> green: EMERALD GREEN
> yellow green: PRIMROSE YELLOW or
>   ENGLISH DUTCH PINK

In addition, careful selections of white, black, and earth colors will be necessary. These colors are necessary to complete the palette. They are far less expensive than the pigments from the basic color wheel listed above.

RAW SIENNA   black: IVORY DROP BLACK
BURNT SIENNA
BURNT UMBER   white: PERMANENT WHITE
GOLDEN OCHRE

Colors may roughly be divided into two categories: WARM and COOL. Those colors possessing predominant proportions of blue, purple, or green are soothing to the eye and are referred to as cool. Colors having a predominance of red, orange, or yellow are striking and energetic, arouse emotion, and are warm. Taking these categories to extreme will render them "cold" or "hot." Cool colors have a tendency to lie dormant or lend an illusion of distance to objects, while warm and hot colors pose an excitement that makes them appear forceful and seeming to approach the observer.

It is not unusual in scene painting to add blotches of a warm or cool color to a nebulously colored surface. Not only will visual variety and interest be enhanced, but the temperature of the surface may be strengthened or altered. The painting surface "temperature," combined with supporting texture, will aid the scenery in the establishment of mood for the environment. While elements of line, mass, and color are standard tools of expression for the artist, the scene painter does not have control of the uses of line and mass within his area of responsibility (unless, of course, he is the designer as well). The painter must combine color and texture on the confines of a two-dimensional surface to create his illusions. He can use ranges of color and texture appropriate to our everyday existence or, of course, take the tools to extreme. All effects are gauged in relation to the actor, the human factor. We cannot help but associate visual elements with our own frameworks of existence. Should a hospital be a deep yellow green stucco environment or a soothing light mint green with smooth walls? Should one create suspicion or serenity? Should a fireplace reveal crisp ceramic tiles or seasoned orange brown bricks? These questions of visual expression are fundamental to the overall conception of the designer, but the matter of execution and knowledge of color and texture must finally be assumed by the painter. The use of temperature in color, combined with illusions of texture, are the keys to the visual expression controlled by the scene painter.

4. Mixing and Liquefing Dry Pigments

To produce almost all types of scene-painting techniques, from texturing to detail work, a minimum of three values of one color are used. This applies to all types of paint, regardless of their medium, and is not restricted to dry powder pigments. Remember, however, that to effectually mix powder pigments, the mixing and combining of color is performed in a dry state. Only after the desired colors are attained should they be liquefied.

Before beginning, one cardinal rule of color mixing must be recognized: IT IS ALWAYS EASIER TO MAKE A COLOR DARKER OR MORE INTENSE THAN IT IS TO MAKE IT LIGHTER. Surprisingly enormous amounts of white are needed to lighten a color that is too dark. Many times it will behoove the painter to empty the spoiled or too-dark a color into an "ends" bucket for use as a back-painting color than to waste voluminous quantities of white in attempts to lighten a dark color.

The three values of color we are to prepare are labeled according to their purpose. The first color to mix will represent the predominant color the scenic unit is to be painted. It is called the BASE COLOR. From this are conceived the two remaining colors: the TINT and the SHADE. In synonomous painting terms the tint may also be called a HIGHLIGHT, and the shade a LOWLIGHT.

Referring to the Table of Nine Mixtures, exclude mixtures 1 and 9, as they represent the absolutes black and white. The middle of the scale, or 4 to 4 ratio, represents the medium or BASE gray. Those colors approaching the absolute white are tints or high(er) lights of the base: working toward absolute black finds the shades or low(er) lights of the base color. For simplicity in the mixing and liquefying of powder pigments, let us use the gray scale of the Table of Nine Mixtures.

Step 1: In the center of the three buckets, add 4 equal parts each of black and white; stir until a medium-gray powder is achieved. Degrees of brightness or richness in producing tints and shades will vary depending on the nature and style of the painting technique. (For average textural or detail work usage, the *middle values* of each of the three tints and shades on the mixture table will suffice.)

18

Step 2: Use the bucket on the left to mix the shade. Mix 2 parts white with 6 parts black. Use *smaller units of measure for the tint and shade* colors, as fewer quantities of these are needed than the predominant base color.

Step 3: Into the right bucket combine 6 parts white to 2 parts black to form the tint.

Step 4: Making sure the SIZE WATER is workable and of the correct consistency, add enough of it to the powder pigments to create a paste. Stir slowly, attempting to eliminate any lumps. Some pigments such as Italian blue and hues of green, purple, and red are stubborn and do not mix readily with other pigments. A couple of drops of denatured alcohol or methanol added to the mixture will break the suspension. Begin adding more size water until the approximate consistency of milk is obtained. Lift the stir stick out of the bucket of color. The liquid should run from the stick smoothly, not in little drops. Beware of too much size water in the mixture. Translucency will result. Too little size imparts too thick a coating of paint that eventually will crack. The paint should be opaque, spread easily, and not be sticky or difficult to spread and blend.

Being powder pigments suspended in size water, all mixed paints should be stirred frequently when in use. If allowed to set, the paint sediment must be dug up from the bottom of the bucket before the color is applied. Failure to maintain a well-mixed solution will result in an uneven application consisting of thin spots and clumps of sediment. Dry pigments do not have a particularly long life after liquefication because of the gelatin glue binder properties. Adding 1 capful of FORMALDEHYDE per 2 gallons of paint will increase its life and maintain freshness for about one week. This extension can be doubled if each bucket is sealed by covering their tops with plastic (POLYETHYLENE). Add a bit of LYSOL or OIL OF WINTERGREEN to counteract the formaldehyde and keep the odor of the paint pleasant.

While mixing the base, tint, and shade of gray by means of the nine-mixture table is no more than a simple cookbook recipe for the inexperienced painter, practice will provide shortcuts to the meticulous measuring process. It is wise for the novice painter to begin early to develop and strengthen an ability to match existing colors. A simple beginning would be to mix the base, tint, and shade grays according to the table, and then abandon all tools of measurement other than the judgment of the eye and attempt to visually match the three values made by the table formula. The easiest way to achieve this is to first mix the base color. Remembering how easy it is to darken colors rather than lighten them, fill a bucket 1/2 full with white pigment. Slowly add SMALL amounts of black until the exact value of the table base gray is reached. Now create the tint color using the method used by most painters. Fill the tint bucket with white pigment, to about 1/4 full. Slowly add portions of the BASE COLOR to the white until the table tint is matched. Uniformly working from lighter to darker tones, put some of the base color into the third bucket to the 1/4 level. Very sparingly add bits of black until the value of the table shade is reached (fig. 8). NOTE THAT

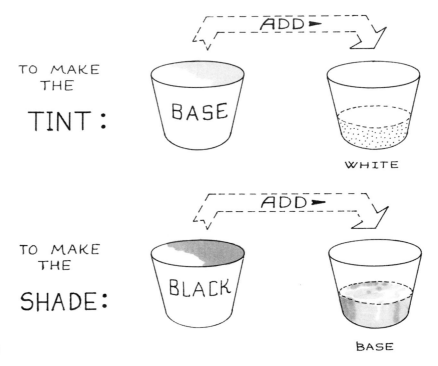

TO MAKE THE

TINT :

BASE

ADD ►

WHITE

TO MAKE THE

SHADE:

BLACK

ADD ►

BASE

Figure 8

BOTH THE TINT AND SHADE WERE MADE BY DARKENING LIGHTER COLORS. Using the base color to make the tint and shade is easier than the table mixture method.

Imagine the base color is not a simple medium gray but a complex green-blue green (an expansion of the twelve principal hues located between green and blue green on the color wheel). One can, of course, pull out the table mixture recipe or proceed as above using the base color pigment as the common ingredient in the tint and shade.

This common ingredient or root color principle can be extended to allow two colors that would normally be repulsive side by side to compatibly coexist. Suppose that for some reason green and purple were required to appear onstage in close proximity to one another. The duo can be rendered ANALOGOUS if an identical additive is introduced to each of them. Examining the properties of purple and green will show that blue is a color found in each. Mix up a batch of white tinted with blue and add equal quantities to equal amounts of purple and green. What will occur is that the blue white will act as a COMMON DENOMINATOR and render the two extreme colors analogous. Carrying this theory further, virtually any color can exist with any other color provided they have been neutralized by a like root. In essence, the formulation of tints and shades derived directly from a base color is basically the same theoretical procedure.

All of the above examples of color mixing have been illustrated because of their simplicity. The theories are quite simple, provided the colors are kept relatively uncomplicated. Sophistication and expertise come with practice, observation, and patience.

5. Preparing the Surface to Be Painted

Before the actual scene painting may begin, some painting surfaces may need a PRIMER COAT. Priming is best defined by listing its purposes:

1. Helps tighten new canvas or muslin and therefore creates a firmer surface upon which to paint.

2. Seals the weave in the fabric, thus creating an even matte surface and helps eliminate light leaks.

3. Seals raw or unpainted wood surfaces. (Untreated or unsealed surfaces absorb more paint than a surface that has been primed.)

4. On older scenic units and flats, priming with a medium-neutral color will help cover previous coats of paint. (Particularly when painting with dry pigments, previous coats of tenacious Italian blue, for example, have a tendency to bleed through subsequent coats of a weaker,

less dominant pigment if a primer coat is not used as an intermediate step.)

The best "binder" for priming is the one recommended for sizing (shrinking and tightening the material) the coverings of new flats: gelatin glue. Mix the priming a little thinner than one would normally mix a paint consistency by using *whiting* with the size water instead of a colored dry pigment. However, add a dash of color to the primer so that it will stand out against the white canvas or muslin.

Check to be sure that all staples or tacks on the flat's surface were thoroughly pounded in when the flat was covered. Raised staples will catch the brush, collect paint, and cause annoying drips in later stages of painting. Using a primer brush or the widest lay-in brush available, work the mixture well into the material. The brush strokes should go in many directions (as in cross-hatching), somewhat resembling a crude figure-eight pattern (fig. 9). When painting a large area, solicit help. If painting alone, work in rough squares and work continuously. Do not

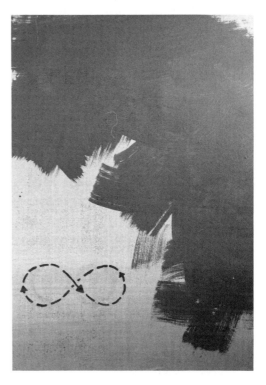

Figure 9

work in haphazard patches and have to go back and fill in spaces. Because the animal glue binder will dry rather rapidly, never stop priming until the entire surface is completed. The idea is to paint quickly to allow the entire surface to dry in unison. Failure to do so will cause uneven tightening and shrinkage of the fabric. If possible, allow the scenery to dry continentally for the even distribution and absorption of the primer solution. A thicker mixture made with stronger size water should be used on coarse, heavier weights of canvas and wood surfaces.

6. Basic Scene Painting and Texture

After the primer coat has dried thoroughly and no thin spots or "painter's holidays" are discovered, the actual scene painting may begin. Some painters prefer to take their base color and apply a base coat as a further sealant. This step is an optional one and is dependent upon the condition of the painting surface, the covering power of the primer coat, and the preference of the individual painter.

The first step in the painting of scenery is to do the LAY-IN work. Covering the surface with the base color alone or with its corresponding tint, shade, or temperature color, constitutes the lay-in stage. Several techniques of texture may be performed during this initial step, or the painter may restrict his application to simple background toning.

Scenery is rarely, if never, painted using only one value of one color on a given surface. Nuances in tone or brightness must be incorporated not only to approach a realistic appearance but also to lend visual interest. In addition, stage lighting is generally strong in intensity and coming from so many different directions that it has a tendency to flatten out even three-dimensional objects and will cause large, flat surfaces to look dull, uninteresting, and reflective.

When a plain, one-colored surface, such as a wall, is studied in daylight or under artificial light, subtle variations in tone often occur near the edges and corners. While such delicate shadings are greatly minimized outdoors, owing to reflected sunlight, interior shadowy areas are intensified conversely because of the lack of ambient light. The room in figure

Figure 10

10 is depicted under daylight conditions with bright sunlight streaming through the window. Notice the wall with the window is the darkest, and the wall opposite the lightest. The source of light is singular and must illuminate an enclosure. The shadings that appear in the corners and near the ceiling create shape and visual interest. As stage lighting cannot solely duplicate these variations in tone, the effects must be applied with paint. Even in stage settings depicting an exterior scene, some degrees of toning must be applied to break up the static appearance of large surfaces.

Regardless of theories of light source and reflection, the common practice in painting scenery, be it for interior or exterior settings, is to paint the top of the scenery darker than the bottom. In interior settings the gradation of tones is strengthened more than its exterior counterpart, and recessed corners are darkened. This is done not only to combat the flattening effect of stage lighting but also to prevent the eye of the spectator from being drawn to bright areas and drifting upward and away from the players. Unimportant areas of scenery should be made to fade away into shadows, particularly those areas high above the actors' heads. Extensive brightly lit detail in insignificant places is most distracting and does not adhere to the fundamental purpose of scenery: to support the action, not distract from it. The scene painter must be aware of this general rule. Many stage settings, regardless of the quality of the design, may be made or broken by the merit of its scene painting and adherence to the role of a supporting element in the production.

The initial step of painting is the laying in of color, in an effort to tone or texture the scenery. TONING is the process of applying a base color with its corresponding shade and tint in order to reinforce the shape of the scenic unit and maintain focus to a specified area. Moreover it is a term used synonomously with "breaking down" or taming a visually distracting element or characteristic of the scenery. TEXTURING shares the responsibilities of focus and combating of light glare with toning but takes a step further to *simulate three-dimensionally textured surfaces*. While individual painters discard, adapt, or conceive numerous methods of rendering texture on scenery, there are twelve common methods of painting texture that serve as the foundation for all variations:

> graded wet blend
> scumbling
> spattering
> sponging
> stippling
> rag rolling
> rolling
> flogging
> puddling
> dry brushing
> stenciling
> spraying

As will be illustrated in part 2 of this book, it is certainly not uncommon to employ more than one, if not several, of the above techniques on the same scenic unit. Study will prove that particular techniques are enhanced when used in association with another method. As an example, one would be hard pressed to find an example of the graded wet blend that was not treated with a subsequent technique. ALL METHODS ARE ILLUSTRATED USING SIMPLY A BASE, TINT, AND SHADE.

Graded Wet Blend

This method is the basic one for accomplishing a soft, linear blending of color values. While the term "wet blend" may refer to any number or

method of brush stroke procedures, the intention with the *graded* wet blend is to produce an even progression of tone from light to dark.

Roughly divide the area to be painted into three horizontal sections, the middle of which is slightly larger than the other two. Lay in a top band of shade fairly heavily and quickly. Do not be stingy with the amount of paint applied, as it will be blended later and must still be wet. Below this, lay in the larger band of base color, again quickly and heavily. Finally, paint in the remaining band with the tint color (fig. 11a).

Now go back with a clean, moist brush and gently feather the edges of one color band into another (fig. 11b). Lastly, take a wide lay-in or pri-

Figure 11a

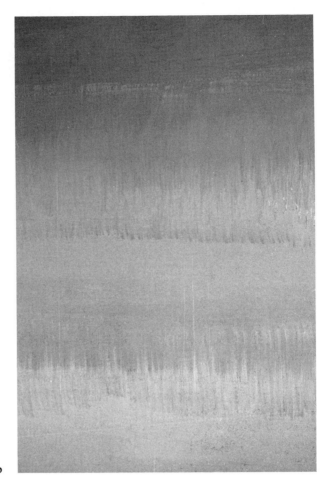

Figure 11b

mer brush slightly charged with water and, pressing firmly, start at the shade end and paint strokes in the direction of the bands of color. Proceed quickly through the base area with continuous strokes, not lifting the brush from the surface until you work your way off the other end of the flat (fig. 11c). If necessary, repeat this procedure with a clean brush and work from the opposite direction. Never work from the middle band out. To paint a flat whose edge will form a recessed corner, simply vary the shape of the top band of shade and arc the following bands of color (fig. 11d). The common follow-up texture for the graded wet blend is normally a fine spattering or spraying.

Figure 11c

Scumbling

Scumbling is used to simulate rough textures such as plaster or stucco and, with minimal distances between the values of the base, tint, and shade, an attractive and lightly textured background for wallpaper stenciling. With this painting method in particular, the extent of the textural illusion is directly related to the contrast in value of the three colors and the amount of blending performed. That is, if one were to mix the tint and shade colors further toward the extreme ends of the mixture table, the impression of rough texture will be intensified.

Figure 11d

Though the rule "dark at the top, lighter at the bottom" still applies, the scumbling painting stroke varies greatly from the graded wet blend. Having a brush for each of the three colors is a necessity to assure clarity of color tone. Smoothe in the shade area, leaving a somewhat irregularly shaped bottom line (fig. 12a). Immediately lay in the base color area, bringing contrasting strokes of the shade into the base and the base into the shade (fig. 12b). These strokes are achieved by quickly twisting the wrist and lifting the brush OFF the painting surface in between every stroke. Leaving the brush on the surface between strokes will not produce the crisp stroke pattern indicative of the painting method. DO

29

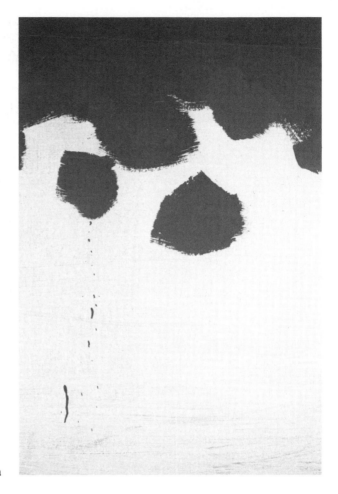

Figure 12a

NOT OVERWORK THIS MINGLING OF COLOR as it will only turn muddy. A splotchy, irregular appearance is desirable.

Continue with the tint color, occasionally exchanging with strokes in the shade area for added contrast. In addition, bring occasional strokes of shade into the tint area (fig. 12c). (A fourth, or "temperature," color can be introduced to heighten the textural effect and add a degree of coolness or warmth. The temperature color has as its common denominator a bit of the base color to which has been added a temperature-producing hue.) Scumbling, like the graded wet blend, is usually a foundation technique upon which further methods are applied.

Figure 12b

Spattering

Perhaps the most widely used method of texturing scenery, particularly by the novice painter, is spattering. Some incorrectly refer to the technique as "splattering," which carries with it a rather uncontrolled and sloppy connotation. Spattering is the act of flicking droplets of paint from a brush onto the painting surface. The brush may be struck against the palm of the hand or piece of wood, or be snapped by sharply flicking the forearm and wrist as a unit. Spattering can be heavy, medium, or fine in reference to the size of droplets distributed (fig. 13a). Droplet size is

31

Figure 12c

controlled primarily by the amount of paint on the brush, but it can also be affected by the distance of the brush from the painting surface and the angle of the stroke. One should consistently change the direction of spattering to avoid discernable patterns. An inexperienced painter must first test his ability on an extra flat or section of the paint room floor. It is more easily performed by the beginner when done continentally where the dripping and running of paint droplets are not a possibility.

Spattering makes use of the base, tint, and shade, and the entire surface is covered with each color. A fourth, or temperature, color is optional and dependent on effect requirements.

To achieve a smoothly textured surface, all spattering should be *even* and *fine*. Figure 13b illustrates a flat that has been scumbled and finely spattered. To simulate a rougher surface, medium and heavy spattering is applied in uneven patterns. Accordingly, more of a contrast in the scumble values supports the nature of the spattering employed.

Should scenery be too bright, spattering is an excellent toning device, particularly when done with transparent colors (glazes/washes) or dyes. A variation of conventional spattering is the "spatter and drag," which can be performed while the scenery is vertical, though continentally is preferred. Fine spatter a small section at a time (approx. 4 by 4 ft.). Before the droplets have dried, wipe them in one direction with a piece of muslin. (A larger area can be covered using the continental method, then dragging the droplets with a clean dust mop or soft push broom.) Because a definite linear pattern is created, this technique works well to enhance wood graining where a linear look is desirable (fig. 13c).

Sponging

Sponging is useful for duplicating plaster and stucco, rough stones, and performing necessary toning or touch-ups when the set is installed

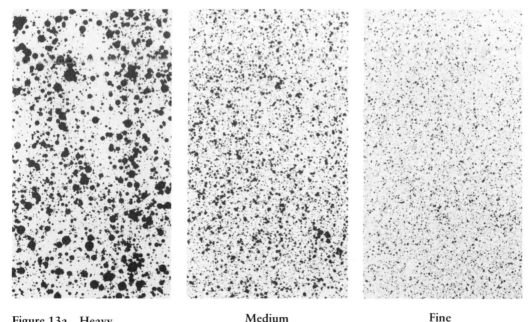

Figure 13a   Heavy   Medium   Fine

in the theatre. Use a large, *natural* sponge because of its unusual, interesting shape and irregularly sized pores. Artificial sponges can be used but are handier where definite shapes or patterns are needed. What is desired is an overall feeling of texture void of overly distinct characteristics.

Immerse the sponge into a bucket of color, squeeze out excess paint, and pat it gently against the surface, continuously changing the position of the sponge to avoid patterns (fig. 14a). Sponging makes use of base, tint, and shade colors with a fairly even distribution of each. For maximum texture and visual interest, sponge a surface that has been previously scumbled. It will provide a unique alternative to spattering (fig. 14b).

Sponging need not be a procedure restricted to texturing. Figure 14c

Figure 13b

Figure 13c

shows a section of painted wallpaper. The lay-in work was a light scumble, on top of which a leaf and blossom arrangement was applied with sponges. Artificial sponges of the household variety were cut into specific leaf and petal shapes. By alternating the positioning of the sponges and the colors applied, the pattern will take shape. This is called STAMPING. More deliberate arrangements are possible depending on the needs of the setting. Recognizable leaf shapes may also be applied as one of the final steps in painting foliage (part 3). With sponging, the

35

Figure 14a

possibilities for imprinting objects and patterns on scenery are endless. (Also see part 2, section 9.)

Stippling

This technique can be quite time-consuming and is sometimes replaced by spattering or sponging. Ordinarily, stippling is done with either of two utensils: the brush or the feather duster.

When using a brush, be sure it is one with blunt-ended bristles, not a

36

Figure 14b

chisel point. The paint is applied by pushing the ends of the bristles against the painting surface from a perpendicular direction. Use a dabbing motion and exert little pressure as only the bristle *ends* should touch. Vary the positioning of the brush while keeping the angle of approach constant (fig. 15a).

The second method is far more expedient. Dip only the end of a feather duster into the paint, squeeze off the excess, and press the feather tips lightly against the surface (fig. 15b). Rotate its position and overlap previous prints between presses. The feather duster method is especially convenient for continental texturing, though avoiding re-

Figure 14c

petitive patterns may be difficult for the beginner. While stippling with a brush is impractical for large scenic units, it is a method perfectly suited to texturing small props, architectural pieces, and furniture.

Rag Rolling

Like brush stippling, this very interesting technique can be inconvenient if used to texture large areas. When done continentally the painter

38

Figure 15a

must work on his knees. Done vertically, the possibility exists of having savage drippings of paint. Procure a piece of 18-inch-square canvas, muslin, or burlap and dip into a color. Squeeze out and then roll over the painting surface using the palms of the hands and varying the rolling direction (fig. 16). Repeat with other texturing colors and fresh pieces of fabric. Rag rolling creates a close cluttered effect and can be used as a base texture. It will usually require a fine spattering afterward as a toning device.

Figure 15b

Rolling

As the name implies, a paint roller is the tool used. Rollers are available in a variety of widths and shapes, while the roller covers come in several degrees of thickness and texture. Roller handles, whether of wood, plastic, or metal construction, can be screwed onto specially made extension poles or the average push broom handle. In addition, paint trays specifically designed for rollers and metal grids for skimming off excess paint are essential roller aides (fig. 17a).

Rolling is an easy and efficient way to paint platform tops and ramps or any large flat area. The speed with which surfaces can be covered is unbeatable. But one can also produce many effects with the roller by varying the angle of stroke, the plushness of the roller cover used, and the pressure exerted. For example, using a thick shag-type cover with little paint is an excellent way of applying a stencil pattern. Exert enough pressure to lightly charge the scenery with paint, and the result will be a texture somewhat resembling stippling and sponging (fig. 17b).

Moreover, discernible or amorphous patterns of texture may be achieved by wrapping wire or wire mesh tightly around roller covers in different configurations. Also try cutting away sections of roller "fur" (fig. 17c).

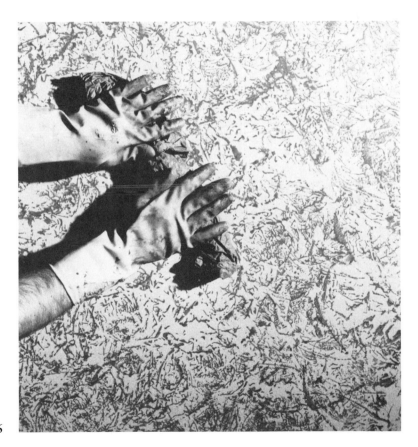

Figure 16

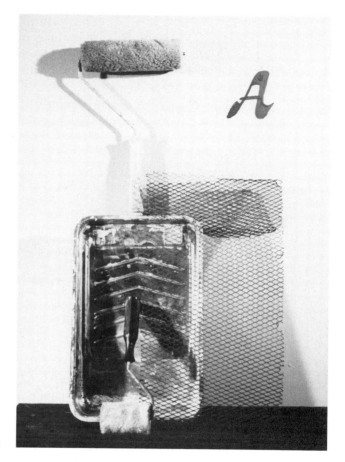

Figure 17a

Flogging

Though used primarily for veining effects and creating strata in stonework, flogging sometimes uses dyes to effect a stylized treatment for foliage and nondescript backgrounds. It is a technique, however, that requires energy to perform.

Secure several canvas or muslin strips of approximately 2 feet in length to a wooden handle. This is called a flogger. Soak the strips in a color, remove the excess, and, holding the handle, "whip" the strands against the scenery. Vary the force of the impacts (fig. 18a). By flogging a second time with water, a soft bleeding effect will result. (The flogger can also be used to remove chalk snap lines or charcoal sketchings that may be left when a painting is complete. Hitting the strands against the dried painting surface, the flogger will beat charcoal and chalk off the surface without rubbing it into the fabric.)

For heavily veined stonework (see part 2, section 8—"Marble"), tie three to four lengths of 1/4-inch wide material in an arbitrary arrangement. Toss the strands gently and randomly against the surface. As the paint is discharged, a nice variety of veining will occur (fig. 18b).

Puddling

Puddling is a wet-blend exercise where spattering of contrasting colors is performed onto a base coat that is still wet. This technique must be done *continentally*. Further variety may be achieved by spattering the base coat with water *after* the spattering of colors, or by spattering hold-

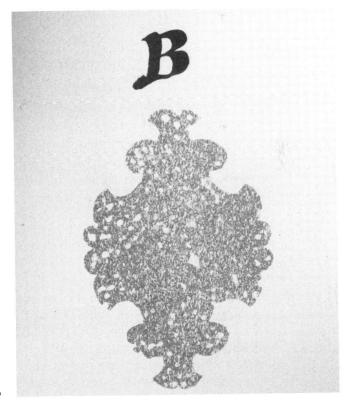

Figure 17b

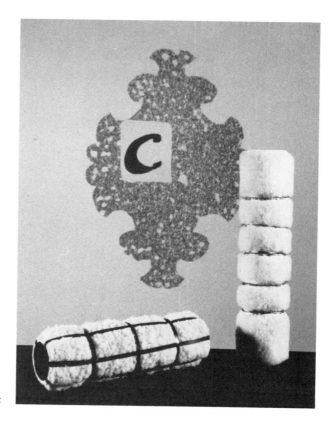

Figure 17c

ing two brushes in the same hand while each brush is heavily charged with its own color. Soft and bleeding pools of color will be produced. Puddling is an especially effective technique to use for producing marble (see part 2, section 8—"Marble").

Dry Brushing

Dry brushing has many uses but is most commonly used to suggest wood graining. The brush, lightly charged with paint or dye, is skimmed across the dry painting surface. (It may help to imagine the brush to be a plane gently landing and coasting down the runway.) Thin lines will result, while twisting the brush slightly will provide interesting variations (fig. 19a). If dry brushing over a moist surface, a softening of the graining characteristics will occur.

Using the cut bristle brush illustrated in figure 6, a form of dry brushing known as COMBING can be achieved. Strokes may be one-directional or perpendicular to produce a woven, clothlike appearance (fig. 19b).

Stenciling

Stenciling can be listed as a method of texturing because it breaks up large expanses of scenery by providing visual interest and a dimension of depth through the nature of its patterns' colors. The most frequent use for stenciling is in the reproduction of wallpaper patterns and floor

Figure 18a

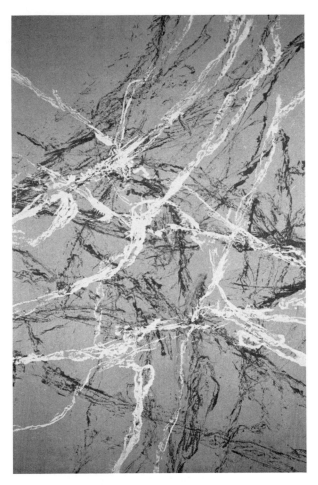

Figure 18b

mosaics, though any repetitive entity (e.g., bricks of a brick wall) may find their beginnings with the stencil.

Stenciling employs oiled stencil paper, sheet plastic, metal grillwork, plastic lace, or any article whose negative spaces (cutout areas) form a design. (If only bristol board or illustration board is available, treat them with shellac or enamel spray paint to seal the paper and help repel moisture [fig. 20].) Paint may be rolled, stippled, dry brushed, sprayed, sponged, or spattered through the holes according to the effects desired, time permitting, and method of painting (vertical or continental).

When painting wallpaper, the stenciled pattern will most likely be of a color that contrasts with the background painting. It will be necessary to mix a base, tint, and shade for the pattern. Separating the degrees of

46

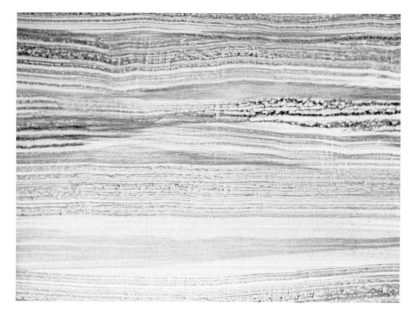

Figure 19a

Figure 19b

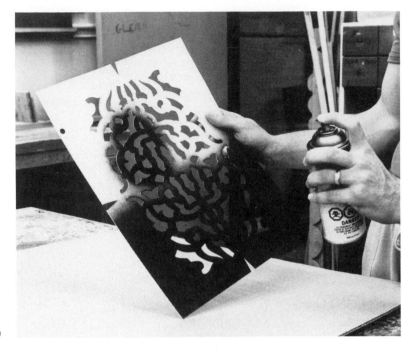

Figure 20

AEROSOL SPRAYER

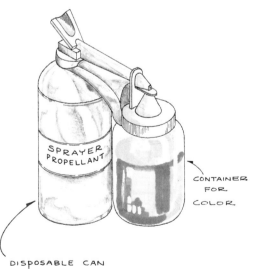

Figure 21

SPRAYER PROPELLANT

CONTAINER FOR COLOR

DISPOSABLE CAN

value will cause a thickly textured look to the pattern (e.g., flocking). The design would never be painted solidly through the stencil, as it would become "heavy" and distracting and thus need further texturing. An *evidence* of wallpaper is all that is necessary (see part 2, section 9).

Spraying

Spraying is very useful for rendering clouds, duplicating fine spatter, and, in short, any painting job requiring a feeling of airiness or subtle gradings and blendings of colors. Stenciling and general toning and shading may easily and effectively be done by spraying. One may use an electric air compressor, hand pump (Hudson) sprayer, or aerosol sprayers, which are available at artist supply shops. Aerosol sprayers

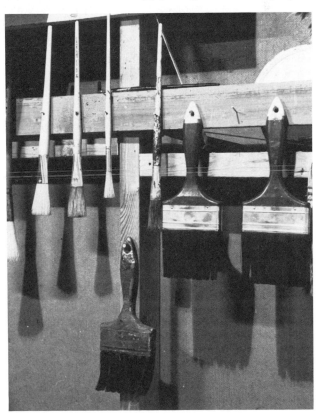

Figure 22

(fig. 21) feature a disposable pressurized power unit and sprayer head with a handy removable jar to house the paint or medium of your choice. With most commercial spray cans (found in hardware stores) the paint inside is enamel, and suitable tints and shades of a color are not available. (Enamel is hard to cover. Most water based paints will bead when applied over it.) Spraying is usually applied finely, in mist form, and layers are built up if heaviness is necessary. The amount of paint applied by spraying is deceiving, however, and it is wise to be done continentally to avoid dripping.

The preceding techniques are fundamental approaches to scene painting and will be abandoned, modified, or even relabeled by the individual painter as he or she moves on to more advanced work. Only through experience and practice will one develop a keen awareness of color and subtlety of stroke. Experimentation will become an ongoing practice as one acquires skill and ingenuity while fostering individual style.

Just as the diligent painter must patiently refine a technique, so must the painting utensils be encouraged to last. Before leaving, take care to thoroughly clean all brushes and tools. *Never* leave a brush soaking, as the wood will eventually swell, subsequently crack and rot, and in turn will result in a loosened ferrule. There is also the fair chance the bristle will have become permanently bent or misshaped.

Wash a brush gently in soap and warm water until you are certain there is no paint clogged inside the ferrule. Water should run clear when the brush is held upside down under the faucet. Shake out all excess water and shape the bristles. If possible, hang all brushes handle up to dry (fig. 22). Long and satisfactory service will result from the proper treatment of all brushes and scene-painting aides.

Part 2.   **Basic Lessons**

As discussed in part 1, all scenery must be textured or treated in some way to counteract the flattening effect and glare of stage lights. And while scenery should also provide visual interest, it must, as well, furnish information unobtrusively in regard to the locale, era, or economic level around which the play revolves.

Though it is not the writer's intention to expound on the purposes or requirements of scenery, the manner in which the scene painting is handled will make a definite statement either in support of, or against, the play's framework. The scenic designer must as carefully as possible select the visual elements that best support the action as envisaged by the playwright. Eventually, the renderings of those elements will become largely the responsibility of the scene painter. And the painter's job is not an easy one: wood must appear to be stone, fabric is painted to resemble wood, flat surfaces must become multi-leveled and seemingly possess a sense of depth and protrusion.

This then is the goal of part 2: to move on to more advanced scene painting and illustrate how the eye can be fooled. We shall attempt to turn a two-dimensional surface into a three-dimensional illusion.

7. The Three-dimensional Illusion and the Light Source

The fundamental principle creating a three-dimensional illusion is that there must first be a light source from which can emanate enough light as to cast overlapping objects in appropriate degrees of brightness and shadow. Simply put, all objects facing and near the light source will have a brighter cast than those objects not facing it and further away.

Let us take the raised, or protruding, panel shown in figure 23A to illustrate the principles of light source and overlapping objects. The smaller square (a) is mounted on *top* of the larger square (b, or background area). Seen from the side view, the smaller square has a thickness and protrudes from the surface of the background square. Now let us assume the light source (perhaps an electric wall fixture) is emanating from the top right-hand corner of the illustration, as indicated by the arrow (fig. 23B). The thickness edges of the smaller square that face the light source will be the brightest and will, therefore, pick up what is called a HIGHLIGHT (i). As indicated, the top and right edges of the panel will be the brightest. Consequently, those edges that slope *away* from the light source will be darker and will receive a LOWLIGHT (ii). Furthermore, the left and bottom LOWLIGHT edges will cast a shadow representing the thickness of the protruding panel away from the light

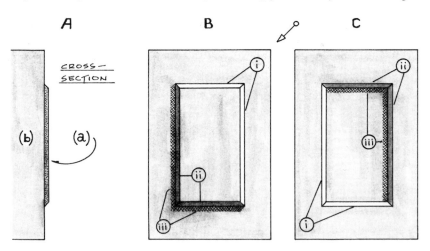

Figure 23

54

source and onto the surface of the larger background square (iii). If a *recessed* panel is desired, figure 23C illustrates the appropriate changes that will occur in highlight (i), lowlight (ii), and shadow (iii) when the direction of the light source is the same as in the protruding panel diagram. Note that whether an object is recessed or protruding from its surrounding area, a shadow will *always* accompany a lowlight and be placed beside the lowlight and away from the light source.

The illusion of three-dimensional squares can be reproduced quite successfully on a two-dimensional surface through proper scene-painting techniques. Until attempting to render curved, angled, or reflecting surfaces, the principles and placements of highlights, lowlights, and shadows are relatively simple ones.

However, choosing or designating a light source is often the tricky problem. Unless there is a designated light source in an interior setting (e.g., a fireplace, lamp, window, etc.), the light should appear to emanate from center stage. Therefore, on stage right the highlighted sides of an object will differ from the highlighted sides of a corresponding object stage left. For example, a raised panel stage right may have its top and *right* edges highlighted, while a stage-left panel will receive its highlighting on the top and *left* edges. Also, horizontal highlights and lowlights will reverse at approximately the six-foot level. Having the light source come from below when an object is placed high on a wall reinforces the realistic attempt at suggesting that a ceiling exists that would prevent the emanation of light from a higher source. Those objects above six feet off the floor will be painted as if the light were coming from below rather than above (fig. 24). Again, this juxtaposing of highlights and lowlights, both of a vertical and horizontal nature, will occur in an interior setting where *the light source has been designated as emanating from center stage.*

Many times a stage setting will contain several light sources of equal or varying intensities. When this dilemma strikes, the scenic and lighting designers must be consulted in order for a dominant or "key" light source to be assigned. Though secondary light sources may certainly be prevalent, it is wise for the beginning scene painter to not confuse the issue and therefore wisely assign one light source for one object to be painted. If, for instance, a window and a roaring fireplace exist at opposite ends of the setting and the three-dimensional painting illusion is to be located upstage center, decide which of the two light sources is the most dominant and use that singular source to create the three-dimensional illusion. As the ability of the scene painter matures, subtleties and

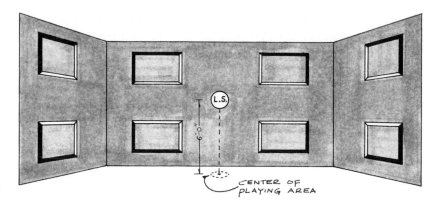

Figure 24

nuances will creep into his or her work that will allow for more sophisticated and realistic treatments of objects appearing under the influence of multi-directional light sources.

It is very unlikely that a room or setting will not contain at least one light source. When that light source is located and assigned, the distribution of highlights, lowlights, and shadows is an easier and more straightforward task than dealing with a setting lacking any plausible light source whatsoever.

Highlights, Lowlights, and Shadows

The colors used for highlights and lowlights are simply a tint and shade, respectively, as derived from the base color the object is to be painted. The tint may contain an additive color reflecting the nature of the light source (e.g., blue moonlight or an orange yellow cast from a brilliant lampshade) if needed to enhance temperature or mood.

The shadow color, unlike the tint and shade colors, should be transparent and allow the surface underneath to show through. Because of its nonopaque nature, such a color is called a GLAZE or WASH. Either term is appropriate and they are used interchangeably. The result and purpose of either are identical.

A shadow wash is made by darkening the lowlight color and thinning it down to a transparency. It should be tested on an extra available surface that has been covered with the base color. The degree to which a wash is thinned is important to the effect desired. When paint is thinned enough for the underpainting to be in evidence, but not clearly so, the

56

wash is TRANSLUCENT. Washes used to create shadows must be TRANS-PARENT, and therefore further thinning of the translucent wash to a transparent state is necessary. Because the wash is primarily tinted water (as in the case of water-based paints), it will be soaked up almost immediately by the previous dry coats of paints upon which it is applied. The danger of applying a shadow wash, regardless of its root medium, is that overlapping strokes will create lines of darker value. That is, each time a wash is applied over itself, its darkness will double and finally, an opaque, dark smudge will exist where the appearance of a shadow should have been. Therefore, when very wide shadows must be applied, either use a brush whose width approximates the width of the shadow's band or use extra caution to place bands of wash directly alongside, and not overlapping, one another. Some painters prefer using aniline dye as a shadow wash because of its inherent transparent nature. Color matching might be difficult for the beginning painter, however, when a medium other than paint is used as a wash.

Lining

Lining is the aspect of detail painting that reveals the shape, contour, and thickness of painted objects. It may be done freehand or with a straightedge as a guide in the same way one would use a pencil and a ruler to outline or illustrate component parts. Most scene-painting lining makes use of some type of guide in association with a brush whether it be a triangle, french curve, template, stencil, or straightedge.

The tools required for lining are liner brushes (or "fitches") of varying widths ranging from 1/4 to 1 inch, a painter's straightedge, large compass, measuring tapes, charcoal and chalk, a bow line or snap line, and, occasionally, a plumb line (fig. 25a). The tapes, snap lines, and chalk are used for the measuring, placement, and initial sketching of the object. According to the geometric scene painting of straight lines and angles, the liner brush and straightedge are used for the application of detail lines. The straightedge is substituted with other templates, etc., as the needs arise. As mentioned earlier, the liner brush has a very definite chisel point to its bristles. Holding its point horizontally while painting with a horizontal stroke will result in a thin line (fig. 25b). Changing the brush to a vertical chisel point will produce a markedly fatter line (fig. 25c), though the amount of paint in the bristles will be exhausted more

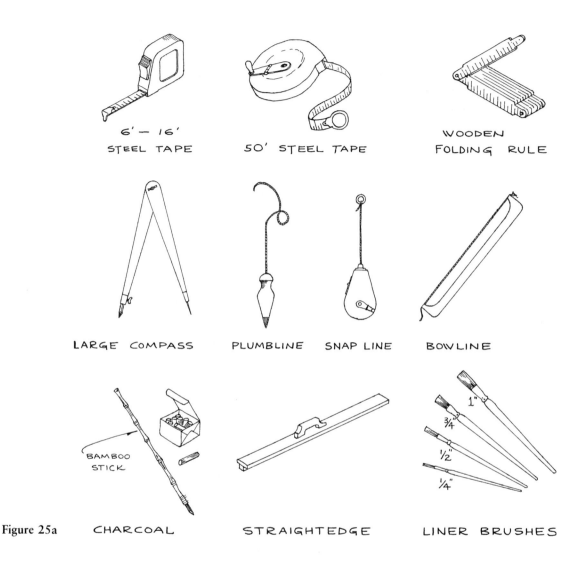

6' — 16'
STEEL TAPE

50' STEEL TAPE

WOODEN
FOLDING RULE

LARGE COMPASS

PLUMBLINE   SNAP LINE

BOWLINE

BAMBOO
STICK

CHARCOAL

STRAIGHTEDGE

1"
3/4"
1/2"
1/4"

LINER BRUSHES

Figure 25a

quickly. Keeping the chisel point in one constant position and sweeping the arm will effect attractive variations in thickness and may be very suitable for script lettering and sign painting (fig. 25d).

The straightedge should have a handle attached to its center. Normally made of pine for a lightweight ease in handling, its bottom edges

58

should have channel grooves to catch excess paint and prevent blotting against the painting surface (fig. 26a).

Hold the straightedge in the left hand while making sure that its top edge is unobstructed by the fingers, thus allowing for the free passage of the brush. Lining should be a rather graceful movement of the entire arm from shoulder to wrist. Keep the wrist firm. Holding the brush lightly between the thumb and forefinger of the right hand while resting it for balance across the edge of the middle finger, let the chisel point of the bristle rest parallel to the surface of the straightedge (fig. 26b). Keeping the handle of the brush at a right angle to the scenery, glide the brush from left to right, nonstop, along the straightedge and allow the tips of the bristles to touch the painting surface. When vertical lines must be painted, simply adjust the procedure 90 degrees using the right-hand edge of the straightedge. Vertical brush strokes should work from the bottom up, however, to minimize the possible dripping of an overloaded brush (fig. 26c).

A little practice will be necessary to exert even pressure along the entire run of the brush. When strokes of even pressure are applied, lines of uniform thickness will result. Conversely, uneven pressure will result in lines of uneven thickness. When running out of paint on a long, straight

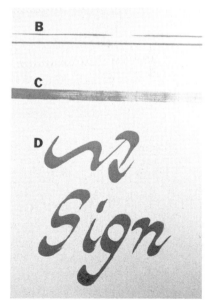

Figure 25b–d

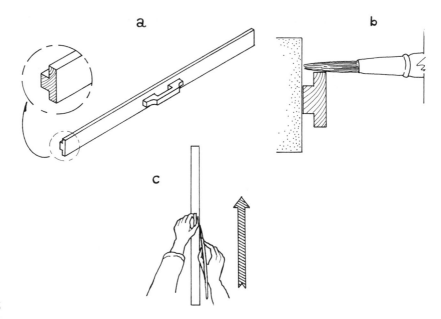

Figure 26

line, recharge the brush and overlap the end of the previous stroke to assure fluidity of direction and pressure. We are now ready to tackle the procedures for painting what may be considered core examples of three-dimensional work. From the following examples, techniques and steps may be augmented or omitted to produce the innumerous variations that are impossible to cover here.

The painting lessons are divided into three categories: stonework (bricks, rough stones, cut stones, marble); wallpaper; and woodwork (rendering methods, wainscoting, recessed and protruding panels).

8. Stonework

Bricks

From the very start, the important thing to remember about bricks is to illustrate some bricks more clearly than others. To illustrate every brick equally on a building or wall would provide too busy or distracting a scenic unit. An overall impression of bricks is all that is necessary. For instance, in painting an aged red brick wall, the painter will want to stay away from the vibrant and dominant reds, yet still capture some sense of warmth. To accomplish this, the lay-in colors will be "browned-down" by adding pinches of burnt umber (blue would be substituted for the brown if a cooler effect is desired). The following lay-in colors of red, deep purple, and orange have now become analogous and will be used to create both definite and vague areas of brick.

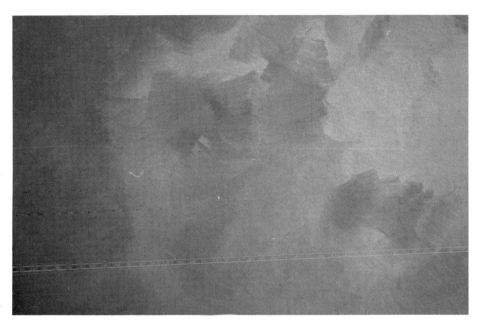

Figure 27

Step 1 (Fig. 27) • Lay-in:

Select and roughly sketch in with charcoal those areas of the wall where bricks should be the most evident. A common practice is to fade in the darkest areas (purple) toward the top and side edges of the flat, thus leaving a nice glow of richer bricks somewhere near the lower center of the painting surface. SCUMBLE in the brightest areas with the red, leaving small accent blotches of orange here and there. The specific arrangement of colors is neither realistically nor artistically regulated. Ac-

61

cordingly, their proportionate area sizes will vary on any two given examples. Lay in the nonessential areas with purple. It is important to note that there should be areas on the flat that are only red, only orange, and only purple in this beginning step. On the edges of these pools of color are where the SCUMBLING occurs. An occasional flick of the brush from the heart of one color into another may be done, but these strokes should be *limited* or muddiness will result.

Figure 28

Step 2 (Fig. 28) • Spatter:

When the previous step has dried, fine to medium SPATTER is applied using all three of the base colors. Be careful not to spatter too much orange, particularly in the purple areas, as this will attract focus by its extreme contrast and thus defeat the purpose of the purple color.

Step 3 (Fig. 29) • Mortar:

Apply the mortar color, which is a medium gray containing a very slight additive of burnt umber for warmth. Begin by horizontally LINING

62

Figure 29

to delineate the bricks. If the rows of bricks have not been chalked or snapped in first, keep the widths of rows of bricks uniform and level by stepping back occasionally to inspect the work from a distance. Endeavor to lessen the pressure of the liner brush when approaching the dark areas, almost to the point of dry brushing. This will create a fading away of the mortar color into the unobtrusive brick sections. Apply the vertical mortar lines and phase out appropriate areas as well.

Step 4 (Fig. 30) • Brick Lining:

Because bricks should protrude slightly from the surface of the mortar, it is necessary to lend a dimension of thickness to the bricks. Mix a tint and shade of the base red. For practical purposes of instruction, again assume the light source to be coming from above and to the right. Therefore, line the top and right edges of the bricks with the tint (HIGH-LIGHT), while the opposite edges are lined with the shade (LOWLIGHT). Do not highlight and lowlight every brick, but note that an occasional brick in the dark area has been lightly highlighted. Randomly vary the thickness of highlight and lowlight lines, as the intention is to suggest an

Figure 30

aged wall where the edges and corners of several of the bricks have become chipped.

Step 5 (Fig. 31) • Brick Dry Brush:

Using a 2-inch brush or a fantail, lightly DRY BRUSH a few random bricks with the base red, orange, or purple. Use only one dry brush color on any given brick.

Step 6 (Fig. 32) • Shadow Wash:

Apply the shadow wash on some bricks to reinforce their dimension over the mortar and dab in some strokes on the faces of particular bricks to suggest uneven surfaces.

Step 7 (Fig. 33) • Final Toning:

Lightly SPATTER with purple any mortar lines that sharply contrast with an underlying purple-based area. Follow this with a final SPATTERING of

64

Figure 31

Figure 32

Figure 33

the entire surface with shadow wash to lend texture to the mortar lines. (Note the graffiti done with blackboard chalk.)

Alternative Method:

As is prevalent in technical theatre, there are usually several means by which to achieve a goal, and methods of scene painting are not exceptioned. Perhaps as popular as the method illustrated above, and preferred by many scene painters, is the painting of bricks using a stencil (fig. 34a).

The laying in of the mortar color is the first step. Base the surface with a gray that has been toned with either blue or brown for temperature. When dry, the mortar is spattered with shadow wash or a tint and shade of the mortar color. Next, spatter, spray, dry brush, sponge, or roll the chosen brick colors through the stencil. Using a thick shag paint roller and applying varying degrees of pressure will result in interesting textural variations. Individual bricks are selected for highlighting and lowlighting and dry brushing. A final spattering with the darkest brick color might be necessary to phase out and tone down areas (fig. 34b).

66

Figure 34a

Figure 34b

Rough Stones

Rough stones are irregular in size and shape and can be done most effectively with a natural sponge.

Figure 35

Step 1 (Fig. 35) • Mortar Base:

Mix a mortar color and base in the entire surface. When dry, SPATTER with a tint and shade of the mortar color.

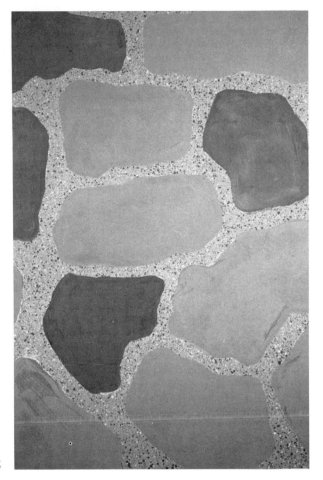

Figure 36

Step 2 (Fig. 36) • Stone Lay-in:

Draw the stones with chalk. Using the base stone color, lay in all stones with the natural SPONGE.

Step 3 (Fig. 37) • Stone Detail:

Randomly SPONGE with a temperature color. Keeping in mind the direction of the light source, SPONGE on the highlights and lowlights with the

Figure 37

tint and shade. Alternate the positioning of the sponge and vary the shape and size of the tint and shade applications, thereby reinforcing the irregularity of each stone.

Step 4 (Fig. 38) • Shadow Wash:

Using a liner brush, follow with the shadow wash and accentuate thicknesses and shapes of stones with shadows cast on the mortar. Finally,

Figure 38

SPATTER the entire work with shadow wash. Refrain from medium or heavy spattering, as this will only flatten the stones' appearance.

Cut Stones

Cut stones are those stones frequently found on royal buildings, monuments, banks, churches, etc. They differ from rough stones in that

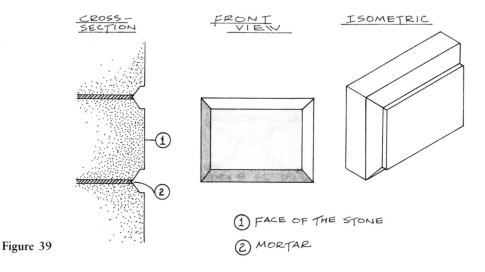

Figure 39

① FACE OF THE STONE

② MORTAR

they are shaped by man and reveal a chiseled edge. Consider a cross-sectional view of a cut stone. Note the obvious bevel that occurs on all sides and the distance from the face of the stone to the mortar (fig. 39). Most commonly made of granite or marble, both of these materials can be seen in a variety of colors. For this demonstration, a reddish brown granite will be painted.

Step 1 • Scumble Lay-in:

Mix up a base of burnt sienna with a small additive of red. From this base, mix a tint and shade. To slightly offset the warmth of the brown and for visual interest, mix a small quantity of mint green. SCUMBLE in the siennas, leaving some areas brighter and more prominent than others.

Step 2 (Fig. 40) • Wet Spatter:

While the scumbling of step 1 is still wet, medium SPATTER with the base, tint, and shade, and sparingly with the mint green. The wet scumble will mingle with the spatter droplets and a slight puddling of the colors will occur. Be particularly careful if painting vertically. Dripping is not desirable. (An optional flogging may be introduced here to achieve a veined granite. See "Marble," below.)

Figure 40

Step 3 (Fig. 41) • Dry Spatter:

When step 2 has dried, FINE SPATTER lightly with all four colors. A medium spatter of the shade can be done on the darker areas. This DRY SPATTERING as a follow-up to the wet spattering of step 2 is done to duplicate the muted/coarse textural appearance of granite.

Step 4 (Fig. 42) • Mortar:

Using a deep brown-black as the mortar color, thinly LINE in the individual stones. (You may, of course, use a lighter mortar color, though with dark granites and marbles a dark mortar is advised. Using a light mortar with dark stones allows the mortar to be dominant and appear to jump to the foreground, thereby counteracting the illusion of the protruding, chisel-edged stones.)

Step 5 (Fig. 43) • Highlight/Lowlight:

Determine the light source and, using the tint color, HIGHLIGHT the in-

Figure 41

Figure 42

74

Figure 43

dented perpendicular edges of the face of the stone. Repeat with the LOWLIGHTING on the opposite edges using the shade color.

Step 6 (Fig. 44) • Glazes:

Using a shadow wash, paint in a wide shadow between the lowlight lines and mortar lines. Repeat between the highlight and mortar lines with a transparent glaze (wash) made by thinning the *tint color*. Turn the chisel point of the liner brush to a 45-degree angle when reaching the corner of the stone to establish the beveled compound shape. Additional applications of the tint glaze and shadow wash will intensify the illusion.

Step 7 (Fig. 45) • Engraving (Optional):

If engraving is needed, simply take the tint and shade colors and with the chisel point of a narrow liner brush adhere to the principles of highlights and lowlights as dictated by the light source to produce the recessed grooves.

Figure 44

Figure 45

Marble

Marble can be found in wide and spectacular ranges of color. Of all forms of stonework, it is by far the most exotic. While many visualize marble as a shiny off-white rock, variations of green, ebony, pink, azure, and brown have been used for centuries to enhance architecture and provide attractive and alluring decor. For example, the study of pink marble may reveal shades of blue, green, or purple as enchanting pools or veinings within the stone. To keep such a range of possible colors analogous, first mix some white with a little brown. The outcome should be a very subtle off-white possessing a degree of warmth. Using this as a common denominator, combine in different buckets with red, green, deep gray, and pink. What should result are two distinctively different hues of pink, a unique pastel green, and a warm middle gray. In addition, keep some of the original off-white, and make a reddish brown shadow wash. Once again, these specific colors are not regulated. One need only study the particular marble to be produced, or experiment to substitute appropriate colors as necessary. MARBLE IS MOST SUCCESSFULLY RENDERED WHEN PAINTED *CONTINENTALLY.*

Step 1 (Fig. 46) • Lay-in:

Quickly lay in the area with the darker hue of pink. Apply the lighter pink, green, and gray while avoiding some areas of the dark pink. DO NOT BLEND.

Step 2 (Fig. 47) • Water Spatter:

Immediately follow with a fine SPATTERING, or spraying, of water. A mottled effect will result.

Step 3 (Fig. 48) • Color Spatter:

PUDDLE the colors further by spattering on top of the water with all colors. Vary the spatter from heavy to fine, but do not cover the entire surface equally with every color. You may choose to spatter again with water, slashing across the painting surface with each snap. (When puddling colors on scenic flats, be careful to avoid soaking with too

Figure 46

much water. It will accumulate between toggles and literally form puddles that will take very long to dry and look dreadful.)

NOTE: While all of the above are drying, cut four to five pieces of heavy twine or thin muslin strips to approximately 3 inches in length. Arbitrarily tie the ends and middles of the lengths together to resemble a loosely woven net. Some long ends should be left untied and hanging free. This device is a "veining net." When step 3 is dry or slightly tacky, dip the net into water to soften it. After wringing it out, dip into a chosen bucket of color.

78

Figure 47

Step 4 (Fig. 49) • Veining:

Dip the veining net into the dark pink, remove the excess color, and toss or FLOG the net gently onto the painted surface. The strands will discharge paint as they strike the surface and produce the veining common to marble. Repeat once or twice and proceed to the rest of the colors, including the off-white and shadow wash. Be certain to change the approach and angle of flogging. The resultant veining will never be the same twice. Substituting the net with a feather or edge of a paint roller

Figure 48

will produce interesting variations, but the painter is more apt to fall into repetitive veining patterns. A further fine spattering or spraying with water will soften the veining if it appears to be too harsh.

Step 5 (Fig. 50) • Detail:

In creating the tint for highlighting, decide which of the colors is the most predominant on the painting surface (i.e., the color that singly occupies the most amount of space and makes the overall color statement).

Figure 49

Make a tint of the color and thin it down to a transparent wash. This will produce highlights and still allow previous painting steps to show through. If more opacity is desired, paint over the highlights a second time with the tint glaze to increase the strength of the line. The existing shadow wash will work nicely for lowlighting and can be handled in the same way as the tint glaze for building up degrees of opacity.

NOTE: Rich marble and fine woodwork are often given a dull gloss to increase their luxuriance. To achieve this, a transparent glaze of a glossy nature is applied (GLOSS GLAZE).

Figure 50

Virtually every paint medium except dry pigments has a clear matte or glossy product available. Most are water soluble to allow for the control of gloss desired. Size water may be used over dry pigments as a handy gloss glaze. However, as all gloss glazes will darken the scene painting, experiment with an extra painted surface before glazing to get an idea of the resultant finish. Consequently, areas requiring a gloss glaze must be painted with lighter values of color to allow for the darkening when glazes.

82

Step 6 • Gloss Glaze:

Apply the gloss glaze. Be sure to give just a hint of luster. Too much glare will destroy any attempts at dimension detailing. If the finished, pre-glossed marbling appears too bright, a pinch of color may be added to the gloss glaze as a toning device. Tilting the flat by picking up different corners will allow the glaze to streak or puddle and create variations in the extent of glossiness.

The dripping and streaking of glazes or washes is not restricted to marble and stonework. Called a "Bergman Bath" after its inventor, scene painter Robert Bergman, this technique may be implemented into the painting stages of various exercises, including wallpaper, bricks, and stonework. Adding amounts of aluminum metallic powder in the glaze solution and allowing it to run down the painting surface will also produce an illusion of dampness and trickling moisture, so suitable for dungeons and dank caverns.

9. Wallpaper

To assure symmetry, the use of a stencil or similar device of some kind is compulsory when wallpaper is required on a setting. At one time, a pounce wheel, pounce bag, and thin paper were the tools used to transfer wallpaper patterns to the painted surface. A design was drawn out on the paper and the pounce wheel would follow along making perforations on the lines of the design. This stencil of sorts was then placed on the painting surface and the pounce bag full of ground charcoal was pounded on the perforated lines. Lifting off the paper would reveal a dotted replica of the wallpaper design. It was then hand painted. The procedure was an arduous one that required steady hands and voluminous quantities of patience.

Preparing the Stencil

More recently the art of stenciling has become more sophisticated. To describe the procedure simply, the paint is now commonly applied di-

Figure 51

rectly onto the scenery through the stencil's negative spaces that form the shape of the wallpaper design. Alternatively, using a stencil can be replaced by "stamping" the paint onto the scenery. Synthetic sponges, cut into shapes, are pressed onto the scenery to cast an imprint; or shapes of sponge or thick carpet are glued to a board with handles, dipped into pan of color, and stamped against the scenery (fig. 51). The latter method is extremely effective for fast applications. The sponge and carpet can be cut with scissors, X-acto knives, or, most conveniently, with a band saw.

Stencils, similarly, can be cut out with matte or X-acto knives. Should several copies of the stencil be required, sandwich and clamp sheets of stencil paper between two pieces of 1/8-inch plywood. Trace the original stencil onto the top piece of plywood and cut out the holes with a power saber saw. For those with access to a more thoroughly equipped scene shop, use of a Cut-Awl machine is unsurpassable for maintaining accuracy. The resultant multi-copies can then be placed on continentally arranged scenery, and the many repeating patterns can be simultaneously stenciled.

When the painting is to be done vertically and only one stencil is used at a time, it would be wise to frame the stencil. Framing not only maintains rigidity but will also prove a handy way to hold the stencil when using it.

To frame a stencil. Cut four pieces of 3/4-by-3/4-inch pine to the lengths required by the dimensions of the stencil. Remember to allow in your calculations for the width of the wood. Arrange the pieces as shown in figure 52a. Place the stencil facedown onto the wood pieces and staple through the paper into the wood using 1/4-inch staples (fig. 52b). Carefully nail the frame together with 1 1/2-inch finishing nails. Finish by brushing shellac on both sides of the stencil and frame to seal against moisture absorption. Note that center guidelines have been notched into the top, bottom, and side edges of the stencil paper just inside the frame (fig. 52c). These notches will be aligned with the horizontal and vertical chalk lines normally snapped onto the painting surface to serve as guides for the placement and positioning of the stencil.

There are thousands of variations of single and combination stencils

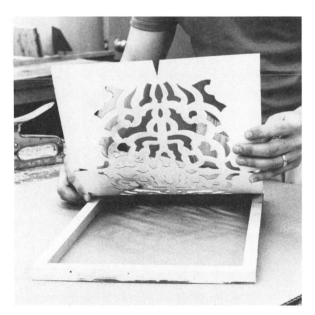

Figure 52a

Figure 52b

Figure 52c

that could be employed for scene painting. For research and quick access, it is wise to stock the paint shop with a few wallpaper catalogues and to keep an extra copy of each stencil constructed for reuse or reference. But this section is not devoted to the creation of a stencil; rather the focus is its application. However, a few hints may prove worthwhile when choosing a stencil pattern:

1. Never choose too large or too small a pattern. Either is annoying. Dependent of course on the size of the theatre and audience proximity, the small pattern will generally read like indiscernible mush; the large stencil will appear too large and stylized and will, therefore, take focus. The average individual stencil design will cover a gross area of approximately 10 by 12–14 inches.

2. Be sure the stencil is not terribly busy. This will carry the same consequence as an overly large stencil. If, however, an intricate pattern is your preference, try creating the pattern in overlay form. That is, break the stencil down into two or three stencils that, when placed one on top of the other, will complete the design. Do the initial shape in one color and use analogous colors for the subsequent stencil intricacies.

3. Make the pattern durable. It might be used a hundred or more times on one setting. Between all cutout sections are the bridges, or ties, that hold the stencil together. Allowing these ties to be too narrow may result in the stencil falling apart. Leave at least 1/4 inch in width for the ties. Accordingly, be careful that there are enough ties and that no long or floppy sections exist.

Before applying the stencil, the background should be textured to provide an interesting contrast to the stencil. The background may be lightly scumbled, sponged, or combed. The method used for the background should be a personal choice related to the appearance desired. It is important to note that *the background texture should be done with washes or opaque hues close together in value*. Its purpose is to contrast and enhance the stencil without detracting from it. Having prepared the background, we apply the stencil.

Applying the Stencil

Step 1 (Fig. 53) • Guidelines:

Snap in vertical and horizontal guidelines. (You will have already chosen how the stencil is to be placed, e.g., side by side, in vertical columns, offset, in diagonal columns, etc.)

Step 2 (Fig. 54) • Stencil Base:

Apply the stencil base color by dry brushing, sponging, or as desired. Work the dominant, or bright, background areas first and apply the de-

Figure 53

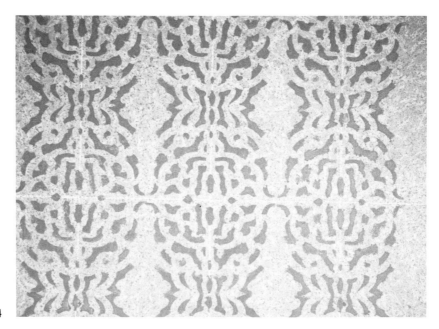

Figure 54

88

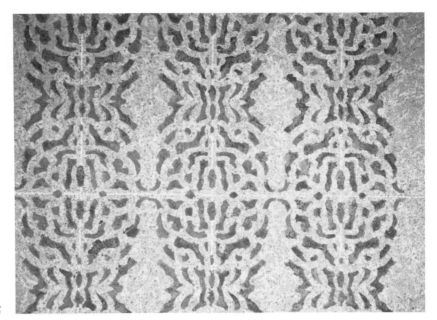

Figure 55

sign rather heavily. Gradually fade out the stencil when approaching the top of the scenic unit and its darker background areas.

Step 3 (Fig. 55) • Stencil Contrast:

Apply the stencil tint and shade colors using the same or contrasting method employed for the base color. Use the tint and shade lightly so as to not totally cover the base color. Vary the placements of the tint and shade colors to avoid static repetition and create stencil texture.

Step 4 (Fig. 56) • Final Tone (Optional):

Finish with a light application of one of the background colors over the finished stenciling by combing, fine spatter, etc. This not only provides further texture but serves as a toning device for too dominant a pattern.

NOTE: Be sure to have made a few extra stencils. When a set is painted vertically, in its assembled form, the extra stencils may be cut in half or in sections for painting the pattern into and around corners of

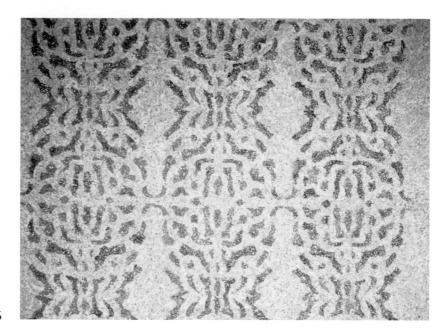

Figure 56

the walls. A quick way to create striped wallpaper is with simple spattering, done either vertically or continentally. Onto a 6-foot-long piece of 1 by 3 inches, perpendicularly attach 6-inch-wide-by-8-foot-long pieces of upsom board or 1/8-inch plywood, at a distance of 6 inches apart (fig. 57a). Having completed the background painting, lay the template on the continental scenery, or in the case of vertical scenery rest the 1-by-3-inch piece on the top of the flat and allow the strips to hang down. Spatter with the base, tint, and shade wallpaper colors. Remove the template and move to the next section of scenery (fig. 57b). Further optional treatments might be the application of a second different template over the background or applied stripes, framing of the stripes with a wash or opaque color, etc.

Remember that unless dictated otherwise, all objects onstage will need some degree of painted or applied texturing. Wallpaper is no exception. Whether stenciled or stamped, the design pattern must be treated with contrasting tones, be they merely tints and shades, to create texture.

90

10. Woodwork

Before attempting to paint any type of woodwork, research the exact wood you wish to reproduce. Study its graining patterns and changes in color. Note if the texture is close and smooth or coarse. Though the examples in the following painting lessons are of a wide-grained nature (such as poplar or pine), variations in color, blending, and graining can be suited to the particular characteristics of the type of wood desired.

The following demonstrations are divided into three categories: rendering methods (descriptions of the three common methods of reproducing a wood effect), wainscoting (the most basic of all interior treatments for decor), and paneling (in which multi-leveled decor is illustrated).

Rendering Methods

Regardless of the complexity of the assignment, reproducing wood-work onstage may take the form of any one of the following three ap-

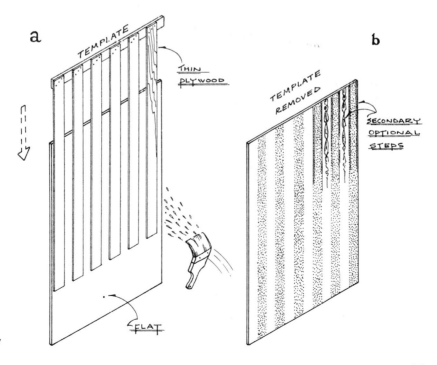

a TEMPLATE THIN PLYWOOD FLAT

b TEMPLATE REMOVED SECONDARY OPTIONAL STEPS

Figure 57

Figure 58

proaches: 1) the wash method, 2) opaque method, or 3) dry brush method. While it is not uncommon for all three methods to be used on the same painting project, dividing and illustrating the techniques into three separate approaches will simplify the procedures for the beginning painter and possibly encourage the adoption of an individual format that has proven comfortable and workable.

Wash Method

Step 1 (Fig. 58) • Neutral Base:

Base in the entire woodwork area with an off-white appropriate to the

Figure 59

temperature of the wood to be produced. When dry, use a felt tip marker to delineate the divisions of boards.

Step 2 (Fig. 59) • Graining:

Add the appropriate graining (based upon research and/or commercially available swatches) with a liner brush and a semidark shadow wash.

Step 3 (Fig. 60) • Washes:

As befitting the type of wood desired, brush on washes of color in the same direction as the graining, and lightly blend. The graining should show through subtly.

Figure 60

Step 4 (Fig. 61) • Spatter/Drag:

Finely spatter with the shadow wash and drag immediately in the direction of the graining.

Step 5 (Fig. 62) • Highlight/Lowlight:

Add highlights and lowlights to the edges of each board to clarify the arrangement and lend a thin beveling.

Step 6 (Fig. 63) • Gloss Glaze:

Finish with a gloss glaze to deepen the tones and add richness.

94

Figure 61

NOTE: Many painters prefer reversing steps 2 and 3, as they feel the blending will provide a more varied foundation for interesting and non-repetitive graining patterns. However, remember that wood is recognized not only by its color(s) but also by its uniqueness of graining. While reversing steps 2 and 3 may free up the style of the painter, such an approach is more suitable to the creation of woody "appearances" rather than a more accurate duplication of a specified wood.

Opaque Method

This second method will be illustrated by rendering aged barn wood because of its many subtle colors and coarse texture. Close inspection of

Figure 62

the unpainted barn wood will reveal both warm and cool tones, however slight, that have resulted from the exposure of the wood's natural moisture patterns to the elements of weathering.

Mix up a base of medium gray and a corresponding tint and shade. For variety and temperature, also mix a reddish brown and a gray blue, using the base color as a common denominator additive.

Step 1 (Fig. 64) • Base Streak:

Base in the entire area QUICKLY and HEAVILY with the base gray. While the base is still wet, dab and streak the tint, shade, brown, and blue *in the intended direction of the grain.*

Figure 63

Step 2 (Fig. 65) • Wet Blend:

With a wide lay-in brush partially charged with water, blend while pushing well against the surface.

Step 3 (Fig. 66) • Inking:

After step 2 has dried, ink in with shadow wash the divisions of the boards and graining lines. Note the tapering characteristics of the grain controlled by the liner brush's chisel point. (Most barns were constructed of the softer woods such as poplar, pine, and spruce because of their ease in handling, availability, and cost factor. Accordingly, the graining is free-flowing and loose.)

Figure 64

Step 4 • Texture:

Dry brush or comb with WASHES of the tint, base, and shade colors.

Step 5 (Fig. 67) • Spatter/Drag:

Fine spatter with the shade and drag ONLY CERTAIN AREAS, leaving what will appear to be nail and worm holes.

Step 6 (Fig. 68) • Highlight/Lowlight:

Using the tint and shade colors line in the highlights and lowlights to distinguish edges of boards and apply shadow wash as needed for di-

98

Figure 65

mension. (Do not apply a gloss glaze, as it would work against the natural and exposed appeal of this type of wood.)

Dry Brush Method

Because dry brushing is largely associated with wood and TEXTURE, this relatively simple third method is best suited for illustrating coarse exposed wood rather than a sophisticated and finished interior treatment. Moreover, in an attempt to capture nature's raw beauty, the following example makes use of rather romantic temperature colors of a complementary nature. Take note that a section of profile scenery is being

Figure 66

painted for this lesson, and while the scenery is still two-dimensional, the perimeter shape will reinforce the nature of the painting technique.

The one distinct advantage this method has over the previous two is that its procedure may be followed as available time permits. There isn't the rush to complete wet blendings or the dragging of colors before they dry.

Step 1 (Fig. 69) • Base/Comb:

Base the entire unit with the warm gray color and allow to dry. Then dry brush or comb the gray blue TRANSLUCENT wash following the directions of the boards.

100

Figure 67

Step 2 • Warm Wash:

Determine the light source and follow with the gray orange wash. Work in sections and do not completely cover the gray blue. Keep the gray orange predominantely, but not absolutely, near those edges facing the light source.

Step 3 (Fig. 70) • Tint/Shade:

Apply the opaque light gray tint and the opaque brown gray shade to add dimension. Do not use a straightedge. These lines should be freehand and have varying thicknesses to capture the nature of the roughly hewn profile cutout.

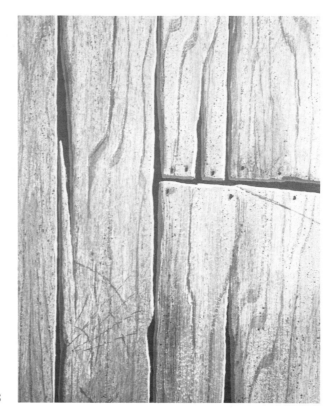

Figure 68

Step 4 (Fig. 71) • Shadow Wash:

Paint on the shadow wash to reflect the overlapping construction. Finish with a fine to medium spattering of shadow wash to give the highlights texture.

It is occasionally necessary to suggest wooden units that have been "painted." For example, not all baseboards or door casings in interior settings will be unpainted. They may be color-coordinated and complement the wallpaper, or offset dark walls by providing a lighter trim. However, though covered with a particular color, such architectural features are still constructed of wood. In such cases where the woodwork has to appear as if painted over, base paint the wood with the chosen color. Now, what you will want to do is create a *sense* of the material.

102

Figure 69

That is, acknowledge that an architectural feature is made of wood, without heavily illustrating its obvious characteristics. Therefore, mix tint, shade, and temperature colors fairly close in value to the base color. Thin these to a transparent wash. LIGHTLY AND SPARINGLY dry brush or comb with all three over the base color. Too little is better than too much. Finish with a gentle gloss glaze as a standard interior treatment.

Wainscoting

Wainscoting can refer to any type of wood paneling on an interior setting, though it is traditionally confined to the lower sections of walls. Characteristically, wainscoting contains a chair rail and a baseboard

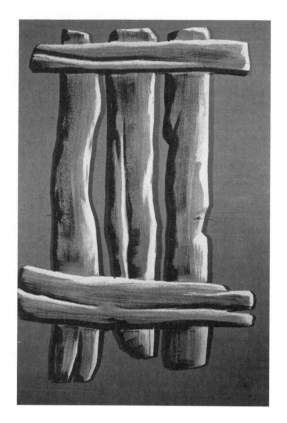

Figure 70

(fig. 72). Notice that both the chair rail and baseboard are applied onto the surface of the paneled area and their grains are predominately in a horizontal direction. In actual construction the area exposed between the chair rail and baseboard runs the full height of the wainscoting and is located between the chair rail and baseboard and the wall; and while both the chair rail and baseboard may assume a highly decorative form, their main purpose is to protect the wall from the gouging and chipping caused by chair backs and legs. Wainscoting may be quite opulent in its design, but as illustrations of intricate paneling are soon to follow, this painting series will showcase the traditional tongue and groove type. The tongue and groove form of wainscoting with its vertical graining was the most popular and modest style of paneling employed for over a century, beginning as a staple of interior decor as early as 1840. Its clean lines and sturdy workmanship reflect a simplicity and honesty

104

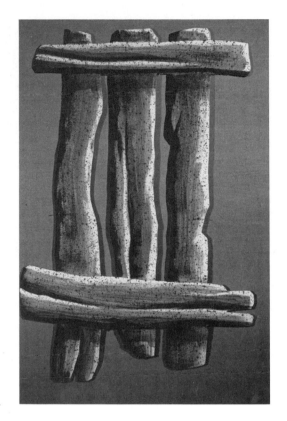

Figure 71

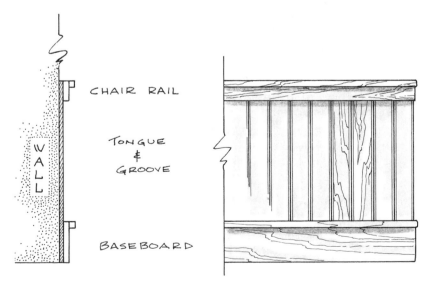

CHAIR RAIL

TONGUE
&
GROOVE

WALL

BASEBOARD

Figure 72

Figure 73

that graced town halls, church basements, saloons, and unpretentious parlors.

Step 1 (Fig. 73) • Ink/Base Blend:

On the side vertical edges of the painting surface, place marks to indicate the widths and positionings of the chair rail, tongue and groove, and baseboard sections. Base and blend all areas according to grain direction. With a felt tip marker ink in the borders of the chair rail and baseboard, and delineate the individual tongue and groove boards.

Step 2 (Fig. 74) • Graining:

Apply the shadow wash graining.

106

Figure 74

Step 3 (Fig. 75) • Texture:

Dry brush or comb with translucent washes of base, tint, and shade.

Step 4 (Fig. 76) • Lining:

Determine the light source. Referring to the cross-sectional view in figure 82, line in the horizontal highlights and lowlights of the chair rail and baseboard.

Step 5 (Fig. 77) • Lining:

Apply the tongue and groove highlight and lowlight lines. (The edges of

Figure 75

these boards have a very slight beveled angle. Therefore use a liner brush with a very crisp chisel point.)

Step 6 (Fig. 78) • Spatter/Drag & Shadows:

Carefully apply a fine spatter and drag (the spatter and drag may have occurred after step 3, if preferred) with the shadow wash. Apply the cast shadows with the shadow wash.

Step 7 • Gloss Glaze (Optional):

Brush on a dim gloss glaze if desired.

NOTE: It is essential to note that all paneling, mouldings, and wain-

Figure 76

scoting are applied onto the surface of any given wall. *Because one should always paint what is farthest away first, any wood treatments must be done AFTER the other background areas of the wall* (e.g., stucco, wallpaper, etc.) *have been painted.*

Recessed and Protruding Panels

Creating paneling more intricate than the conservative tongue and groove wainscoting is in actuality no more difficult than painting cut stones. Where the assignment begins to take on more complexity is when curved or multi-angled surfaces must be rendered. A review of the painting exercises thus far will reveal projects of simple geometric lines

Figure 77

that were strictly horizontal or vertical in nature and met at 90 degree corners. The only true deviation has been the cut stone where rather wide beveled surfaces came into play. As you will recall, because such surfaces do not directly confront the light source, attempts to render them utilized washes of tints and shades that produced medium-range tints and shades, or half-tones. In essence, middle grounds between the tint and base or shade and base were achieved by singular or repeated applications of the transparent washes.

Painting 90 degree-oriented paneling of an intricate nature will also make use of washes simply made from the tint and shade colors. The recessed and protruding panels in figure 79 illustrate highlight (1), low-light (2), and shadow wash (3). The procedures used were a combination of the wash and opaque methods. Note the distinct variations

110

Figure 78

in thickness of the tint, shade, wash, and shadow wash lines so as to enhance the illusions of depth and protrusion. Also, the panels have been given added interest and distinction through the use of diagonal blending.

Additional examples of woodwork—lattice (fig. 80), clapboard siding (fig. 81), and board and batten (fig. 82)—are fundamental treatments found in innumerable settings depicting exteriors of homes.

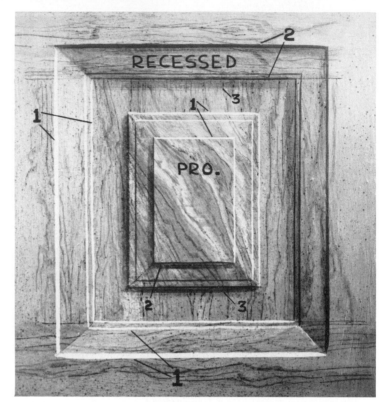

Figure 79

Figure 80

Figure 81

Figure 82

Part 3. <u>Advanced Lessons</u>

Part 1 of this book discussed the materials and tools of the scene painter and primary methods of texturing scenery. Part 2 dealt more specifically with basic demonstrations on painting stonework, wallpaper, and wood-work. Part 3 will introduce more advanced work as we paint cornices, draperies, foliage, reflective metallic objects, scale transfers, perspective vistas, drops and scrims; and it will take a freer and bolder approach to scene painting than parts 1 and 2. The emphasis in part 3 will be away from geometrically oriented and right-angle adjoining of highlight and lowlight lines and toward a more sophisticated employment of half-tones and flash colors. At times the straightedge will be all but thrown away and the artist and his brush will be free to explore on their own.

11. Cornice Moldings

Most moldings and cornices incorporate at least one curve into their structure. In order to properly duplicate a particular shape, cut into an actual molding or draw a cross-sectional view of it. The Roman ogee is perhaps as widely used for decorative cornices as any other design and is by far the most recognizable (fig. 83a). In actuality this popular mold-ing is a combination of three primary shapes: the vertical plane, S-curve,

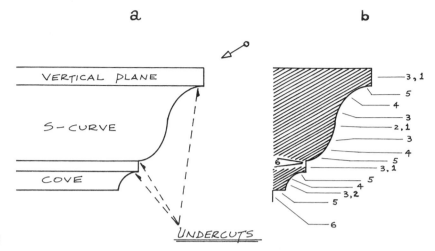

Figure 83

and cove. Further delineation is provided to isolate the "undercuts" and an arrow to indicate the light source.

The majority of moldings can be effectively rendered with six colors: 1) the tint wash; 2) the tint; 3) the base, or local color; 4) the half-tone, or middle shade; 5) the shade; 6) the shadow wash. The preceding numbers applying to the six colors indicate in figure 83b where these colors occur. To elucidate the following demonstration, a profile of the molding shape has been attached to the edge of the painting surface.

Step 1 (Fig. 84) • Inking:

Extend ink lines from the attached profile across the painting surface to show the horizontal delineation of its facets.

Step 2 (Fig. 85) • Lay-in:

The painting is a rather simple blending procedure, provided the colors have not been mixed too far apart in value. Use a separate brush for each color. Start from the top of the molding and work down in horizontal bands. Note, however, that the first two colors used are NOT blended, as they should depict the crisp corner where the top vertical band and S-curve meet (undercut).

116

Figure 84

Figure 85

117

Figure 86

Step 3 (Fig. 86) • Overlap:

Just below the top band where the undercut leads into the curved areas of the molding, overlap the bottom edge of the previous stroke with the top edge of the following.

Step 4 (Fig. 87) • Wet Blend:

With a clean brush slightly moist with water, horizontally blend the S-curve section. Be careful not to use diagonal strokes. What you are in fact doing through the blending is creating a series of gentle half- and quarter-tones.

Step 5 (Fig. 88) • Bottom Blend:

Following the reference diagram (see fig. 83b) complete the bottom and carefully blend the cove section.

Figure 87

Figure 88

119

Step 6 (Fig. 89) • Tint Dry Brush:

When the painting is dry, gently and judiciously dry brush the tint wash on the top vertical band and bottom bulge of the S-curve.

Step 7 (Fig. 90) • Shadow Wash:

Use the shadow wash ONLY where indicated, as it will have a flattening effect if applied to curved surfaces. Touch up with more tint wash if needed.

The molding depicted in figure 91 makes use of a large concave (or cove) pattern with a half-round section toward the bottom edge. The same colors used for the Roman ogee were used here. The widths and placements of the color bands produced the alternative shape.

However, cornice moldings such as the ones illustrated are traditionally located at the *tops* of wall sections where the wall and ceiling meet. If said walls form part of a realistic interior setting, the light source will be coming from below and shooting upward even if a ceiling

120

Figure 90

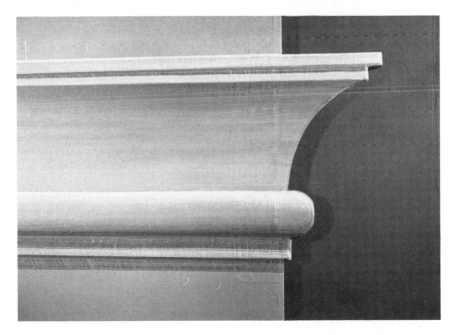

Figure 91

121

is not actually part of the setting. The ogee and large cove moldings in figure 92 have been painted as if the light source were coming from below. The chair rails painted below each of the cornices would normally be located below the six-foot level on a setting and therefore adhere to the basic principle of interior light source placement and are painted accordingly to reflect their placement as being *below* the source of illumination.

Attempting to paint a molding out of marble, where the compelling characteristics of the stone must be in evidence, is a different task altogether and will not follow precisely the steps set forth above. Instead, paint the marble as if it were a flat slab lacking a light source and, consequently, without any evidence of depth or protrusion. Allow to dry and do not gloss glaze. Using a tint and shade of the dominant color in the marble, thin to wash transparencies. Make a sketch of the cross-section of the molding and determine the light source. Remember that to approach translucency with the wash, apply additional coats. When working both the tint and shade washes, have an extra clean brush ready and charged with water in order to blend areas of the washes into the background painting.

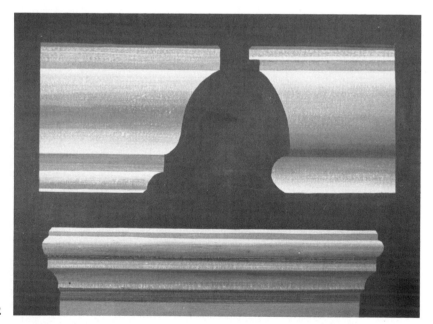

Figure 92

NOTE: If a gloss glaze is to be used on any molding, keep it WEAK. Any reflections resulting from overt glossiness will most surely destroy the illusion of shape you have created.

12. Draperies

Painting drapery is challenging because the bold wet-blending strokes involved cannot be duplicated with the safety and security of the painter's straightedge as a guide. By the very nature of a drapery's gentle folds and artistically gathered pleats, painting drapery requires the rendering of irregular surface contours that must appear soft and inviting rather than stiff, austere, and rigid.

As the process of scene painting is an overlapping one, progressing from the background and building toward the foreground, painted draperies will be one of the last things added to the interior setting. Consequently, if draperies were to cover a french door or window through which can be seen a yard or hillside, the drapery would be the last to be painted, as it will overlay all exterior views and window panes.

Similar to painting woodwork and numerous other objects, a wash method, opaque method, or combination method may be used to paint draperies, depending on the extent and richness of background areas that must be overlapped or opaquely covered. The following lesson will use opaque colors, although the drapery base color has been thinned a little to allow the initial inking to show through. The following itemized colors will be used, though not necessarily in the order listed:

1. drapery base color
2. drapery highlight
3. drapery lowlight
4. fringe base
5. fringe highlight
6. fringe lowlight
7. fringe flash light (tint of highlight)
8. shadow wash

Figure 93

Step 1 (Fig. 93) • Sketch/Ink:

It is imperative to first sketch and ink in the overall shape and arrangement of the drapery. With this example, because the drapery valence hangs in front of the vertical bottom section, the valence will be painted AFTER the lower section. Providing the draperies with some tassels and fringe not only adds to their luxury but also helps define their arrangement.

Step 2 (Fig. 94) • Lay In Base:

Lay in the drapery base color.

Step 3 (Fig. 95) • Lowlight/Wet Blend:

Follow immediately with the lowlight and wet blend sections into the edges of the base color, occasionally using clear water to facilitate the blending.

Figure 94

Figure 95

Figure 96

Step 4 (Fig. 96) • Highlight:

While the previous steps are still moist and tacky, brush in the highlight drapery color, blending some strokes more thoroughly into the base color than others. To increase fold definition, use the highlight as the *base* for the back of the drapery fabric (middle right). Accordingly, use the original drapery base color for shading the drapery back.

Step 5 (Fig. 97) • Valence Base:

Having inked in the valence shape, apply the drapery base color.

Step 6 (Fig. 98) • Valence Detail:

Add the shade of the valence and vary the width of strokes, as this element of drapery is more bunched and pleated than its free-hanging, vertical counterpart. Apply the valence highlight and blend accordingly.

126

Figure 97

Figure 98

Figure 99

Step 7 (Fig. 99) • Fringe & Tassel—Base:

Lay in the fringe and tassel base color.

Step 8 • Fringe & Tassel—Lowlights:

Working in uneven clusters, paint in the fringe and tassel lowlights.

Step 9 • Fringe & Tassel—Highlights:

Apply the fringe and tassel highlights as in step 9. Uniform highlighting will flatten out the folded look of the drapery and will make the fringe appear stiff.

Figure 100

Step 10 (Fig. 100) • Accents:

Using the drapery highlight and fringe flash light on their respective sections, accent contours and areas with quick, bold strokes. Keep the use of these two colors to an absolute minimum and be selective in the areas enhanced.

Step 11 (Fig. 101) • Shadow Wash:

Complete the draperies with cast shadows on and from the tassels, fringe, and valence.

To give a nap or surface texture to the drapery material, gently scumble the strokes during steps 3 *and* 4 with a liner or fantail brush.

Figure 101

13. Foliage

Because foliage is a product of nature and not man-made, it is very difficult to render convincingly. It must look natural, free, and unplanned. The saying "only God can make a tree" is a creed followed by the wise, experienced designer who will assign the painted foliage of a realistic setting to only the farthest upstage areas of a realistic setting. Three-dimensional tree trunk replicas should be used in the brightly lit foreground, while clumps and masses of painted foliage should be supporting elements restricted to the background, or upstage areas. (In fact, painted draperies should also be located far from the audience.) The use of scrims and cut drops are tremendously helpful in creating a wooded scene, as they effect a haze before the more distant trees, add to the illusion of depth, and thus render the painted foliage more convincing. Cut drops are particularly useful for silhouette effects, often by

130

creating a better impression of trees than detailed painting will allow (fig. 102).

Painting foliage employs any number of earth colors and brush strokes, depending on the type of tree to be reproduced. Varying shades of green, in addition to reds or purples, come into play to lend roundness to the overlapping blocks of green. Several tree bark colors will also be used. Devote some time to researching the characteristics of different trees. Study outdoor magazines, calendars, Walt Disney-type books, and real foliage.

These are the colors to be used for the following lesson, though not necessarily in numerical order:

1. purple wash (translucent)
2. dark green
3. middle green (predominant leaf color)
4. light green
5. flash-light green
6. bark base color
7. bark temperature color
8. bark tint

Figure 102

9. bark flash tint
10. bark shade
11. shadow wash

The painting background has been laid in by a graded wet blend that approaches its lightest hue at the chosen horizon (colors for the background not listed above).

Step 1 (Fig. 103) • Sketch/Ink:

Sketch and ink in the tree(s). Brush in any distant trees using only the purple and dark green, thinned to a translucent wash.

Note that there has not been an attempt to render the entire treetop. The area to be painted was isolated, based on the relative size of the painting surface. Attempting to capture the entire tree on such a relatively small area would dwarf its effect, tighten its airiness, and clutter the painting stroke. Because of the enormity of trees in relation to hu-

Figure 103

man size, a tree's full scope is rarely depicted onstage unless pictured in the distance.

NOTE: All objects in the outdoors, regardless of their actual surface colors, will gradually assume a purplish gray overtone as they appear closer to the horizon. By the same token they will become fainter and fainter toward the horizon, and consequently a wash is used to achieve an illusion of objects appearing in the distance, as opposed to an opaque color that will look heavy and pull the distant object toward the foreground.

Step 2 (Fig. 104) • Purple Wash:

With a fantail brush or wide liner brush (depending on the relative size of the tree to be painted) lay in the background foliage of the far side of the tree, using splashes of the purple wash. Allow to dry.

NOTE: Allow bits of sky and background foliage to show through during this and the following steps as you work toward the foreground

Figure 104

Figure 105

of the tree. Failure to do so will lend a heaviness to the tree and render it cluttered and artificial. Too little color is far better than too much. Do not overwork the amount or shapes of leaves.

Step 3 (Fig. 105) • Dark Green:

Apply blotches of background foliage with the dark green. Notice that we have been working up to, and not completely over, the tree branch and trunk lines.

Step 4 • Trunk Lay-in:

Lay in the base trunk color, letting the branches overlap the green and purple masses.

Figure 106

Step 5 (Fig. 106) • Trunk Temperature:

Dry brush the bark temperature color on all areas of the limbs and trunk.

Step 6 (Fig. 107) • Middle Green:

Lay in the middle green color, in some areas overlapping the previous green and again leaving bits of sky to show through. Use this green the most, as it represents the basic leaf color. Be sure to cover sections of the branches and trunk with the middle green. Dabbing at the surface with the sides and end of the foliage brush while changing direction with the wrist will produce a nice variety of leaf contours.

135

Figure 107

Step 7 (Fig. 108) • Trunk—Highlights & Lowlights:

Using a medium-loaded brush, sketch in irregular trunk branch high-lights and lowlights, often drifting into a dry brush stroke.

Step 8 (Fig. 109) • Light Green:

Dab the light green on various clumps of middle green while slightly covering more of the branches. Keep the light green toward the top half of the middle green clusters.

NOTE: Reinforcing the light source (in most cases the sun) on foliage is not a straightforward task because of the high degree of ambient, or reflected, light in the outdoors. One can, however, shift the majority of light and flash-light greens toward a particular side of the tree. High-lights and lowlights on the branches and trunk will greatly assist in es-tablishing the direction of the light source.

Figure 108

Figure 109

Figure 110

Step 9 (Fig. 110) • Accent:

Flick on leafy accents with the flash-light green. Be selective.

Step 10 (Fig. 111) • Shadow Wash/Bark Flash Tint:

Finish the tree with shadow wash on the bark areas and add the bark flash tint to the trunk and branches.

Foliage with recognizable leaves can be painted by stamping. Cut several leaves of a specific design out of synthetic sponges. Follow the painting steps outlined above. When applying the middle green (step 6) use the stamp sparingly on the edges of its masses of color. As the foliage tones lighten toward the foreground, use the stamp more frequently while turning its positioning for variation. Occasionally do a partial print so the leaves will not look as if they are pressed against an invisible glass shield (fig. 112).

138

Figure 111

Figure 112

Trees of all types can be duplicated by varying the leaf and bark colors, angle of the brush print, the positioning and shape of leaves, and the characteristics of the trunk and branches. Always experiment with your technique on a spare surface before attacking the actual painting surface.

14. Reflective Metallic Objects

Metallic objects are difficult to render because of their reflective quality. Principles of light and shadow are thrown out the window when an object is to possess a surface sheen. Therefore, most objects pretending to be metallic onstage are three-dimensionally formed from styrofoam or similar media, primed, and treated with bronze powders. And because bronze powders are available in wide ranges of color, they can be used alone or mixed with paint for the purposes of scene painting. These three-dimensional facsimiles of ornamentation will actually pick up and reflect, to a certain degree, surrounding action and movement.

As is the case of "convincing" foliage and drapery, objects painted on a two-dimensional surface to resemble shiny and lustrous metal are usually placed in the upstage extremities to enhance their illusionary credibility. Even at such a distance from the audience, the scene painting will not be *totally* believable. In fact, it will never really look realistic, and the scene painter should never overconcern himself with photographic realism. If he does, he will never be satisfied with his work, and there will most likely be little enjoyment in it. Though the painter should strive for a sensibility in what he paints, and to an extent a justification of his technique, he must attempt to capture the *essence of characteristics* in what he paints, even at the expense of visually reminding the audience that the stage is filled with scenery and not absolute, real life.

The scene painter cannot hope to discover the definitive method for painting reflections if he merely observes a subject. Unless he remains at one point of observation, he will find that as he moves so will the nuances and almost absurd placements of highlights and shadow.

In painting reflective metallic objects the scene painter should take his cue from the cartoonist. That is, the painter must be bold in technique:

slash on staccato bursts of flash colors and shade; keep experimenting until the essence of a shiny surface is captured. If research must be done, look through the advertisement pages in the newspaper. Study, for example, the ink drawings of stereos and microwave ovens. Observe how insensible configurations of line, simply and magically, create a metallic illusion. Also try studying drawings and photographs of a new car's chrome and attempt to transfer the same techniques into brass-, copper-, and gold-colored similarites.

For the upcoming lesson, bronze powders will be added to the paint colors. First, prepare the powders to a paste consistency by combining them with a little alcohol and a double-strength binder. A clear vinyl binder is the best to use as it will least affect the clarity and brilliance of the powders, as compared with other binders that may dull or change the initial colors. Little by little, add more water until the desired wash consistency is attained. (If used alone, the powders should be brought to the consistency of working paint. When used as a glaze or mixed with paint, a wash consistency is best.) Add the prepared bronze powder solution a little at a time to the already mixed paint. Try out the mixture on a spare painting surface. The metallic powders should float to the surface as the painting dries. Adjust the ratio of bronze powder to paint, if necessary.

The painting object in this lesson will resemble brass. Add amounts of the equivalent bronze powder colors in prepared solutions to the colors of paint mixed:

> base color
> half-tone shade
> shade (deep)
> tint
> flash light
> white
> shadow wash (no bronze powder)

Step 1 (Fig. 113) • Sketch/Ink:

Sketch, then ink in the object and determine the light source. (The object was first drawn on brown paper then transferred by the pounce method to the painting surface.)

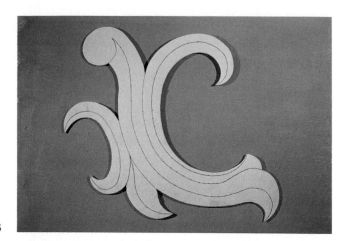

Figure 113

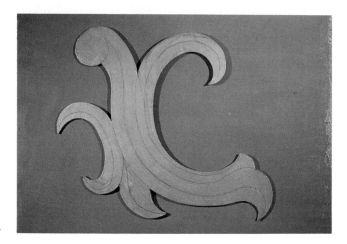

Figure 114

Step 2 (Fig. 114) • Base Lay-in:

Slightly thin down the base color to allow the inking to show through, and base in the entire object.

Step 3 (Fig. 115) • Half-tone/Highlight:

Select the protruding surface edges of the object and, keeping the base coat moist, quickly etch in the half-tone shade the highlight colors on

142

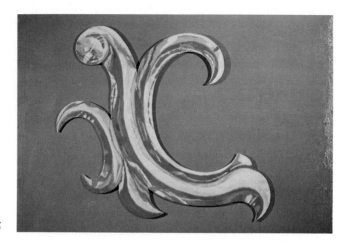

Figure 115

the appropriate sides of the raised edges. Strokes and lines should NOT be of uniform length or width but should taper or blossom accordingly as a curve is approached. Because of its unique reflective quality, metal may exhibit a variety of tones that stop and start abruptly, leave gaps between sweeps of line, or produce dots and dashes of brilliant highlight next to deepest shade. Therefore, lay some strokes of highlight and half-tone *on top* of the base color while lightly blending others in with it. (On large objects, perhaps bits of surrounding scenic units may be painted in to reflect on the object, e.g., a window, dark doorway, etc.)

Step 4 (Fig. 116) • Shade/Flash Light:

The shade and flash-light colors may now be applied in quick, graceful sweeps on top of the still moist previous color. Afterward, when the painting is dry, with a 1/4-inch liner brush dab and dot judiciously with the flash-light color and white to accentuate peaks and high points of particular curved surfaces.

Step 5 • Shadow Wash:

Complete with cast shadows of the object onto the background painting. (You may want to very finely spatter with shadow wash to antique the finish—optional.)

Individual talents and personal preferences will vary and fluctuate

143

Figure 116

from painter to painter. Some have a flair for painting foliage, others for drapery or marble. But by and large, the most difficult surface to render for the average painter is the reflective surface. Each reflective object you paint will have drastically different placements of color, caused simply by variations in the surface shapes and contours. There is no fundamental rule to follow when painting these surfaces, except perhaps the rule common to all forms of scene painting: DO NOT OVERWORK THE JOB. Developing the skill to effectively paint reflective surfaces may take some time, but eventually, you will know when the painting begins to work.

15. Scale Transfers

A scale transfer is a process by which any drawing may be proportionately enlarged or reduced and reproduced on another surface. In the theatre where scale is usually larger than life, the original drawing is most often transferred to a larger scale such as would occur on a scrim or drop. The act of enlarging remains constant regardless of the scope of increase. To increase a 3″ × 5″ drawing to cover a warrior's shield is

144

really no different in principle than enlarging the same drawing to cover a wall. For the purpose of practicality, however, this lesson will illustrate a transfer to a 4′ × 8′ flat.

The sketch to be transferred must be drawn to scale, commonly 1/2″ = 1′0″, and then gridded off with squares. First, overlay the original drawing with tracing paper and tape securely into place. To serve as initial guides draw vertical and horizontal center lines. Working 1/2″ apart, lines are drawn parallel to the vertical and horizontal center lines until the entire sketch is squared off (fig. 117). Each 1/2″ × 1/2″ square, according to scale, will represent a 1′0″ × 1′0″ square on the scenic surface. (*Clear acetate* works the best as an overlay, as it will protect

Figure 117

the sketch from dirt and paint droplets and wipe clean. Its surface is slick and nonabsorbent, however, so the grid lines must be done with *indelible ink*.)

NOTE: An alternative to the grid method of scale transfer is to project the drawing onto the scenery using an OPAQUE PROJECTOR. The painter's elevation is placed in the projector. Assuming adequate space is available, place the projector at a distance from the scenery where the projected image will cover the entire surface to be painted. The design is then chalked onto the scenery. (OVERHEAD projectors may be used if the elevation has been painted with dyes or washes on a transparency.)

Figure 118

When the scenery is to be painted continentally and/or sufficient space to use an opaque projector does not exist, sections of the design may be projected onto brown paper and pounced onto the scenery. The initial chalk lines are corrected and verified by inking with strong dye or felt tip markers.

Step 1 (Fig. 118) • Gridding:

Mark off one-foot intervals on all four sides of the larger surface, again using the center vertical and horizontal points on the larger surface as

Figure 119

initial reference guides. With a charcoal snap line or bow line, grid the larger surface. (If much of the sketch contains an expanse of sky, lay in all of the sky colors first, then grid over it when dry. In this case, notice that the flat has been base painted prior to the gridding with the background sky colors.)

Step 2 (Fig. 119) • Sketch/Ink:

The design is sketched with charcoals sticks (so that mistakes may be dusted or flogged off) and later inked.

Figure 120

Step 3 (Fig. 120) • Painting:

Areas are laid in and detail painting is performed. Done in a monochromatic fashion with opaque colors, this design used in total only five hues of purple. To make the scene appear hazy and distant, the lightest purple (sky base color) was very finely spattered over the entire surface.

148

16. The Perspective Vista

Although perspective vistas can be transferred and drawn by using the grid method of transfer, a knowledge of the basic principles of perspective is an asset. Perspective is the art of rendering an object so as to show a dimension or depth that will increase or decrease in size according to its relative positioning between the observer and the horizon. The simplest example of the effect of perspective is to envision a set of railroad tracks. You, as the observer, are standing between the tracks. Because the two rails are parallel, as they move away from the observer they will appear to converge at a spot on the horizon, or "eye level." This point of conversion is called the vanishing point. Even a child can scratch the horizon line across a piece of paper, draw the crudest of converging railroad tracks, and achieve some degree of an illusion of distance and depth on a two-dimensional plane. The two initial lines, here symbolized by railroad tracks, must, however, in real life have a parallel relationship in order to converge at the same vanishing point.

Other parallel lines, such as those indicating the top and bottom of a building, will meet somewhere along the horizon line and create their own vanishing point. Moreover, two buildings on opposite sides of a street, but facing and parallel to one another, will share the same vanishing point. All lines that are parallel to flat ground and above eye level (the horizon line) will slope *down* to the vanishing point, while all lines below eye level will slope *up* to it (fig. 121).

During the Renaissance, when the science of perspective was markedly advanced and refined, vistas were elaborated to sometimes include three or more vanishing points. Often points were located off the picture plane, or parameters of view. To reproduce such a sophisticated setting through scene painting, one would have to rely on the grid method of transfer alone, as locating actual vanishing points on such a large scale would be impossible because they might occur one hundred yards or more away from the painting surface. But convincing examples of distance and diminishing proportion can be illustrated when only one vanishing point is used. The works of Canaletto (Giovanni Antonio Canal, 1697–1768) will serve as adequate inspiration for those artists who regard one-point perspectives as static and lacking in interest. Canaletto's drawings took on startling complexities because of his use of overlapping objects. Often his vanishing points seem nonexistent for they are most often either eclipsed by foreground and middle-ground fea-

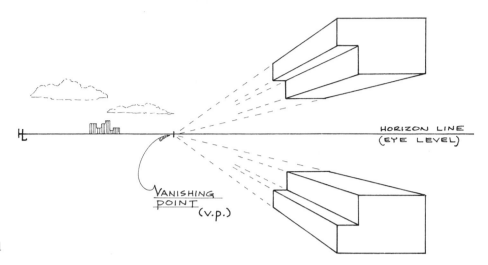

HORIZON LINE
(EYE LEVEL)

VANISHING
POINT (v.p.)

Figure 121

tures that virtually block clean views of the horizon, or occur severely off to one side of the center line.

Perspective works the most convincingly when the observer's view is directly in front of the middle of the picture. In theatre, not all, or many, members of the audience will have seats in the center of the auditorium, however. It is true that viewing perspective from an angle off to one side or another of the central line of sight will tend to lessen the illusionary effect of perspective. But again, scenery should never strive for total realism. For in a realistic vista, should not the leaves in a clump of painted foliage sway? Should not there be *some* distant activity at the end of enormous palace courtyards? In actuality, yes; in theatre, no. Recall the words of Robert Edmund Jones who labeled scenery "an environment of the action." In an attempt to satisfy every audience members' conceivable scrutiny of the scenery, the designer (and painter) will have overstepped the bounds of scenic propriety and given the setting extensive dimensions of importance and focus.

Consequently, to avoid an artistic temptation to achieve convincing realism, it is quite common to see the perspective vista rendered in a seminonrealistic form, e.g., pen and ink etchings, tintype sepia washes, bleeding strokes of dye, etc., in attempts to capture the style of an artistic period or achieve a romantic flavor.

150

It is not unusual for the drawing of the vista on the painting surface to take appreciably longer than the act of painting the scene.

After having gridded the designer's rendering, locate its vanishing point (v.p.). To do this use a ruler or straightedge as a guide and align its edge, first, with the top and, then, the bottom edges of one of the buildings and lightly extend these lines until they cross. Where they meet will be the vanishing point. Mark this point with a dot. (This will also indicate the horizon line if it is not already in view.) In one-point perspective all other buildings on the street may be extended to converge at this same spot.

Figure 122

Step 1 (Fig. 122) • Grid/V.P.:

After the painting surface has been gridded, locate and mark the vanishing point. (The entire surface was based earlier with sky colors.)

Step 2 (Fig. 123) • Perspective Lines:

Snap in all of the perspective lines. If only one person is to sketch the vista he may loop the end of the snap line over a tack nailed into the

Figure 123

scenery at the vanishing point, extend and tighten the other end of the line to the grid reference points with one hand, and snap the line with his free hand. When painting scenery that lacks wooden supports, use a chalked bowline or another person to help snap the lines. All lines may, of course, be dusted off should mistakes occur.

Step 3 (Fig. 124) • Sketch/Ink:

Sketch and then ink in all details.

Step 4 (Fig. 125) • Pale Lay-in:

To maintain the period flavor of this particular vista, only sepia washes of varying hues will be used. Lay in all areas with the pale color.

NOTE: When working singularly with washes and dyes, one must remember that areas and features can only be made darker. To correct mistakes later, one must use a different medium, i.e., opaque colors or bleach for highlighting purposes. Therefore, care must be taken to prevent painting the designated lighter areas with darker tones. A good rule

152

Figure 124

Figure 125

Figure 126

to follow is to always begin with the palest wash or dye and work progressively through the values to the darkest tones.

Step 5 (Fig. 126) • Middle Lay-in:

Apply the middle tone.

Step 6 (Fig. 127) • Dark Lay-in:

Follow with the darkest tone.

Step 7 (Fig. 128) • Highlight/Shadow Wash:

Finish sparingly with an opaque and translucent highlight to complete architectural details. Cast shadows.

NOTE: Do not be afraid to effect textures by the appropriate method(s) of your choice using a color mixed between the middle and darkest tones as the texturing color.

154

Figure 127

Figure 128

17. Drops and Scrims

Many amateur and educational theatres are forced by budgetary restraints to reuse a scenic drop, or same set of scenic drops, year after year. Once a drop has been dyed, even the most energetic cleaning and mild bleaching will usually reveal particular colors of dye too tenacious to evacuate the fabric. So the obvious follow-up to the previously dyed backdrop is to paint it for the next production with opaque colors. Even then, some dyes might "ghost" through the dried paint. And if a drop was first painted with opaque paints, then, of course, all subsequent designs must be done with opaque colors.

But for those lucky enough to attack brand new drops, a basic step must be taken to prepare the fresh fabric for dying or painting. Inexperienced painters will frequently be frustrated by the uncontrollable bleeding of dyes and washes that will occur and spread throughout the weave of the drop. Although designers sometimes call for such a bleeding of color, it is always a preplanned notion and a well-monitored technique. Painters can encourage the spreading of color by wetting the drop with water before, during, and after the application of the actual colors. Regardless of the painting technique to be employed, however, all new scenic drops should be glazed with a *primer of liquid starch*. This will not only prevent the running of colors but also provide a tightly stretched and firm surface on which to paint.

To make the starch primer. Mix 1 pound of GLOSS laundry starch (it will dry to a clear matte) into 1/2 gallon of cold water. The starch must thoroughly dissolve. Stir this mixture a little at a time into 2 1/2 to 3 gallons of boiling water. Allow to cool. (To assess the amount of liquid starch you will need, 1 gallon of the primer will cover approximately 100 square feet.)

Sweep clear the paint shop floor and place lengths of gray bogus paper over an area slightly larger than the drop itself. Overlap the edges of the lengths of paper as they are positioned and tape the ends to the floor to avoid shifting. On the floor paper snap a chalk line indicating where the top of the drop is to be placed. Parallel to this line snap a second line at a distance from the first line that equals the height of the drop. This second line will serve as a guide for the bottom of the drop. Placing a large right triangle (painter's floor triangle) or reliable scenery jack at the left end of the top line, extend the perpendicular edge until it crosses the bottom parallel line (fig. 129). Mark the top and bottom lines at these

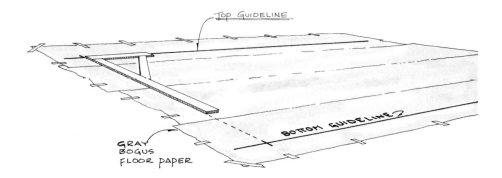

Figure 129

points, remove the perpendicular guide(s) and snap a line to connect the
top and bottom guidelines. This third line indicates the left end of the
drop as seen from the front. Measure from this third line along the top
and bottom lines the same distance as the length of the drop and make
hash marks. Connect these two points by snap line, and the guidelines
for the placement of the drop are complete. Check the accuracy of the
box by measuring from corner to corner. The distance between the
lower-left and upper-right corners should equal the distance between
the upper-left and lower-right corners.

Place the drop on the gray paper, adjust to match the snap lines and,
at intervals of 6 to nine inches, tack into the paint shop floor. If your
floor is not made of wood, construct a wooden frame the exact size of
the drop. (To make the frame, use scrap pine or 3/4-inch plywood butted
and keystoned together to form the desired lengths and assemble by
standard flat construction, replacing the nails on the corner block assembly with screws [fig. 130]. The screws allow for the convenient dis-
assembly and storage of the frame.) Tack the drop to the face of the
wood by first aligning the perimeter of the drop with the outer edges of
the frame.

Strain the starch primer into a Hudson sprayer. In addition, you will
need a soft-bristled push broom and another person. Starting at a top
corner of the drop, work in 4-to-5-feet-wide bands across its length.
One person operates the Hudson (on a medium setting), followed by the

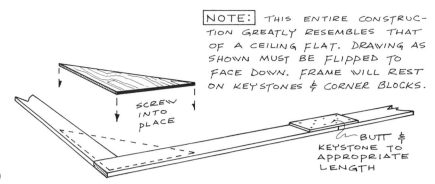

NOTE: THIS ENTIRE CONSTRUC-
TION GREATLY RESEMBLES THAT
OF A CEILING FLAT. DRAWING AS
SHOWN MUST BE FLIPPED TO
FACE DOWN. FRAME WILL REST
ON KEYSTONES & CORNER BLOCKS.

SCREW
INTO
PLACE

BUTT &
KEYSTONE TO
APPROPRIATE
LENGTH

Figure 130

second person who, with the broom, gently spreads the starch evenly
OVER the fabric. DO NOT PUSH the starch into the fabric, as this will
likely cause the solution to pass through the material and be absorbed
into the paper. (It will also cause the paper to stick to the rear of the
drop. As a safeguard for durability and ease in handling, specify when
ordering the drop that you would like one constructed from a heavy-
weight muslin. The thread weave will be close and permeability will be
minimized.) Continue working in horizontal bands until the drop is
completed. A uniform drying time for the entire surface is necessary to
ensure the even tightening of the fabric. The amount of drying time required is proportionate to the temperature and humidity level of the
work area. A warm, dry atmosphere is the optimum condition.

Depending on the manner in which the drop is to be painted, it is
possible to add powdered pigments to the starch primer so as to arrive
at the lightest background color specified on the painter's elevation. All
subsequent steps of applying color, whether a dye or a paint, should follow the tenet of overlapping scene painting: paint first what is in the distance and work toward the foreground. It is advisable to apply the base
coat and background colors and blending (e.g., sky, combing, textural
pattern) before the gridding and charcoal sketching are performed. In
the case of gridding, the painter(s) may find it less visually confusing
when sketching in the design if merely the points where the vertical and
horizontal grid lines cross are indicated rather than the complete lengths
of lines (fig. 131). For quick reference, code by number or letter all vertical and horizontal grid lines on both the painter's elevation and the
drop. The charcoal sketching can then be achieved by gridded scale
transfer, projections, or pounce patterns.

All scenic drops will, at one time or another, have to be rolled, folded,

Figure 131

or tripped. It is quite rare that a drop is painted on the stage floor or paint frame, rigged into position, and then either left there for eternity or destroyed when the production has closed. Most drops are painted in a separate area and folded, and sometimes stored for days before being taken to the theatre. Stages lacking fly lofts necessitate the rigging of roll drops or traverse tracks to operate the drops during scene shifts or to simply clear them for setup and technical rehearsals. Limited storage facilities often cause drops to be improperly folded and bound with string. (The wise technical director will either roll the drop around its tops and bottom wooden battens and wrap it in brown paper or properly fold and place it in a plastic, labeled garbage bag or piece of polyethylene for protection.) The BINDER used with the color medium on the drop must, therefore, allow for these types of handling.

For example, if one were to use the flake gelatin glue as the binder for dry colors, the properties in the gelatin are brittle and do not allow for the flexibility necessary to prevent the cracking of paint or permanent creases that are likely to occur if the drop is rolled or folded. Vinyl, polyvinyl, and latex binders are costly and, though more resilient than flake gelatin glue, are not as suited to the demands of pliable handling as FLEXIBLE GLUE. This rubbery glue comes in slab form and is dissolved in water. The method for preparing flexible glue is similar to the one used in the preparation of flake gelatin glue.

To properly prepare the glue. In a large double boiler, soak 8 pounds of flexible glue in 2 quarts of water for 1 hour. (This will soften and slightly expand the slab[s] of glue.) Then, on a medium-low setting, heat and stir until dissolved. This will produce the liquid flexible glue. (These directions are from the Gothic Color Company, a principal distributor of flexible glue.)

To make the WORKING SIZE. Mix 1 part liquid flexible glue with 8 parts hot water. This binder should be used to liquefy the dry colors (traditional powder pigment, powdered casein, etc.).

Painting the Drop

Step 1 • Background:

Lay in background colors, patterns, or textures (if applicable).

Step 2 • Sketch:

Chalk in all reference gridding and space notations for the scale transfer and cartoon all detail work. Use pounce patterns if necessary.

Step 3 • Inking:

Finalize detail lines and ink in.

Step 4 • Base Colors:

Apply the base colors assigned to specified areas. These colors, unless otherwise specified (e.g., dyes, muted tones, puddled, dribbled, or wet blend patterns), are opaque.

Step 5 • Texturing:

Tones above and below the value of the base colors, temperature colors, and texturing is performed with paints in wash consistencies.

Step 6 • Highlight & Lowlight:

Tints and shades are applied for highlighting and lowlighting; they may be of wash or opaque consistencies. Shade washes will darken and contour efficiently, whereas bright tints or flashes may need to be opaque or reinforced/substituted with bronze powders.

Step 7 • Toning:

Perform a final toning. Dribble, spatter, or spray aniline dryes or paint washes over the entire drop.

A single drop on a stage with a 35-foot-wide-by-20-foot-high proscenium opening will cover approximately 700 square feet of vertical space. Regardless of its size, one can be sure that, related to the size of an actor, the drop will attract a lot of attention. Lighting can help create mood and direct focus to the action, but as a precaution some degree of final texturing on the drop is desirable and often essential to lend texture or simply tone down the painting.

Translucencies

Some drops may contain translucent sections as a part of their design. Directly upstage of the drop is hung a neutrally painted backdrop, or cyclorama. When lights are focused on the neutral drop, a glow will bleed through designated areas of the painted drop. Marquees, signs, lighted windows, and foliage are some examples where a translucency can be effective.

There are two reliable ways to create a translucency. After the drop has been starched and the inking of detail work is complete:

1. Paint the translucent area(s) with a chosen color of aniline dye. After drying, the areas surrounding the translucency are painted with opaque color.

The second method is to:

2. Lay in the translucent sections with aniline dye and cover with hot paraffin. (A convenient container is an old electric coffeepot with hidden heating element. A long extension cord allows the painter to walk to any area on the drop and brush on the hot wax.) After the wax has hardened, paint the drop as planned. Upon completion, scrape off the wax with a putty knife and back-paint the opaque areas.

It is usually necessary to back-paint drops requiring translucent treatment. As a final step the drop is flipped over and the rear of the opaque sections are coated with a dark color (commonly a "slop paint" from a bucket containing ends of mixed colors).

Cut Drops and Scrims

A cut drop is a drop that has had certain negative space areas of its design removed in order to allow for a partial transparency. Areas to be cut out are outlined with aniline dye that has been mixed with alcohol and shellac (the alcohol penetrates the starch primer coat and the inking shows through on the back of the drop). After the painting is completed, the drop is turned over and the designated openings are cut out.

For best results, dyed pieces of *shark's-tooth scrim* are attached to the back of the cutout sections with *flexible glue* (fig. 132). The scrim will act as support for the drop while permitting transparencies to occur through the holes. Bobbinet scrim, scenic netting, or cheesecloth may be used as a substitute, but all are inferior in strength and cannot compare to the opaque/transparent capabilities of shark's-tooth. Cut drops are ideal for an overlapping scenic effect and creating illusions of distance.

A variation on the cut drop occurs when the entire drop or portion of it is glued to a full-size, prepainted scrim. The prepainted cut drop is laid facedown on the floor, all edges are squared and the drop is sparingly stapled to the floor. The scrim is then laid facedown over the cut drop, aligned, and tacked into place. Using a flexible glue, apply through the scrim along the cutout edges of the drop. Apply extra portions of the glue to the sides, top, and, if provided, bottom of the cut drop for a firm adhesion to the scrim. Alternatively, cut drops, or sections thereof, may be applied to the face of the scrim (the scrim is on the bottom, faceup) provided waxed paper is placed between the scrim and the floor to prevent sticking. An alternative to fully sized cut drops or scrims is the use of sections of canvas or muslin, which when combined with pieces of scrim will add up to numerous possibilities for use as border and profile pieces (fig. 133).

When painting a scrim, perhaps the clearest way to lay out the design

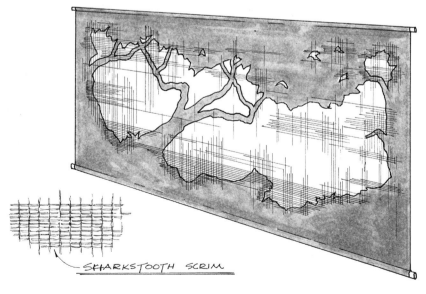

Figure 132

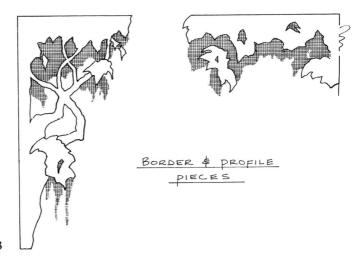

BORDER & PROFILE
PIECES

Figure 133

is to first grid, sketch, AND ink the design on the floor paper (gray bogus). The scrim, which has been starched, predyed, and treated to the background specifications, is laid faceup over the floor paper, aligned, and tacked or stapled to the floor. The inked design will clearly show through the scrim. The procedure of scene painting remains constant whether working on opaque, translucent, or transparent surfaces: apply the background colors and work toward the foreground. Any medium may be used depending on the effect(s)—i.e., degrees of transparency or brilliance of color—desired. Detail lines needing to be completely opaque can be achieved by combining flexible glue or latex with powdered pulp or paste forms of color. The mixture should be kept quite thick and applied using plastic squeeze bottles or disposable cake decorator cones. (To avoid sticking when dry, be sure those areas receiving opaque treatments have been backed with waxed paper.) If soft highlighting is to occur on a scrim or drop that has been DYED, 1 part liquid bleach mixed with 4 parts water can be used to lift off the aniline dye. Should brighter highlights or flash accents be needed, oil paints are the best to use, as aniline dyes will not penetrate them and bleed through to the surface.

Glossary

analogous colors In painting, different colors rendered similar in value because of a common root (denominator) additive.

aniline dye The premiere dyes used in the theatre for scene painting; poisonous, containing extracts of benzene.

animal glue Colloquial reference to gelatin glue, containing animal derivatives that form a tenacious binder for powder pigments.

back-paint The painting of the rear side of scenery with opaque paints in order to eliminate light leaks.

base (local) color The predominant color a piece of scenery is painted; from which are made the tint and shade colors.

binder A substance that adheres the paint to the scenery; term applied to any form of glue used with scene paint.

bogus paper (gray) Commercially available absorbent paper possessing a pebbled texture primarily used as a protective layer between continentally painted scenery and the floor.

boomerang A multi-leveled, rolling unit upon which a painter stands when painting tall vertical scenery.

bow line A chalk line tightly strung on a bowlike piece of wood. The line must be charged with chalk pieces or chalk bag; use according to snap-painting guidelines.

bronze powder Ground metallic powders used widely for ornamental painting; do not contain their own binder.

butt joint Standard arrangement of two pieces of lumber for the purpose of joining; most commonly, end to edge and end to end.

casein A type of scene paint loosely derived from milk protein; durable, in paste and liquid form containing its own binder.

combing A method of texturing using a wide brush missing clumps of bristles so as to resemble the teeth of a comb; an even, linear textural pattern.

complementary color Any two colors directly across from one another on the color wheel.

continental system The act of painting scenery that is lying faceup on the floor.

cool Referring to an emotional mood quality derived from the temperature value of color; any soothing, complacent color such as blue or green.

corner block assembly Element of standard flat construction. Rail and style are butted at 90 degrees, and a right triangle piece of plywood is lapped over the joint and nailed or screwed into place to secure the joint.

cut drop A scenic drop featuring cutout sections that serve as translucencies or transparencies.

drop A rectangularly shaped element of soft scenery usually made of muslin; hangs vertically and is commonly painted as outdoor scenes.

dry powder pigment Oldest and traditional medium of scene paint; needs a separate binder.

eye level Same as horizon line.

fantail brush Scene-painting brush whose ferrule forces the bristles out in a fan shape; used to paint foliage and ornament because of its cutting edge.

ferrule The metal part of the brush located between the bristles and handle; holds bristles in place and reinforces their shape.

fitch A liner brush.

flash color A brilliantly bright tint used for special accenting.

flogger Device used to remove chalk and dust from the painting surface, or to impart a painted texture.

flogging A method of texturing where paint is applied using strands of material whipped against the scenery.

floor triangle A form of painter's straightedge, used continentally to locate and strike perpendicular lines.

foliage brush Same as fantail.

gelatin glue The premier glue of scene painting; excellent when used with dry powder pigments and as a strong and working size; in ground and flake form. [*colloq.*] **animal glue.**

glaze Same as wash.

gloss glaze A glaze leaving a luster when dry.

glue pot That which is used to heat and melt gelatin glue; double-boiler or electric types.

graded wet blend A blending of colors using a gradation of colors; usually an even, linear pattern of bands of color wet blended together.

graining Texture by dry brushing or combing to achieve a wood grain appearance.

grid(ding) Overlaying a drawing or scenic surface with squares for the purpose of a scaled transfer.

half-tone A hue located halfway between the base color and its corresponding tint or shade.

highlight The application of the tint color in an attempt to create an illusion of protrusion.

horizon line The horizontal line where earth and sky meet; the extent of one's visibility of distance, uniformly on the same level as the eye of the observer.

Hudson sprayer Commercial hand-pump sprayer best suited to priming and unsubtle texturing; large and rather heavy, though portable.

hue A quality of color; a particular shade or tint of a color.

inking The verification of a chalk-sketched drawing by using aniline dye or ink markers.

keystone A rectangular piece of 1/4-inch plywood lapped over a butt joint and attached to ensure stability.

Kraft paper (brown) Commercially available nonabsorbent paper used to safeguard against paint spills or mishaps; excellent with the pounce method for transferring detail work.

latex A rubber-based binder and form of scene paint widely used in the theatre.

lay in The application of background or predominant colors prior to formal texturing and detail painting.

lay-in brush A 3- to 6-inch-wide brush used to quickly apply color.

light leak Thinly painted areas revealed by backlighting; usually unintentional.

light source An actual or invented source from which light is emitted so as to create three-dimensional scene-painting effects; that which illuminates thickness and contour.

liner brush A chisel-pointed brush used to produce think, crisp lines and sweeps of varying thickness.

lining The act of detail painting that reveals shape, contour, and thickness.

lowlight The application of the shade color in an attempt to create an illusion of depth.

opaque That which cannot be seen through; any paint that covers and hides what is underneath; opposite of a wash or glaze.

paint carrier A scene-painting aid; a type of box and vertical handle arrangement used to carry paint containers and brushes so as to self-contain painting supplies and increase the mobility of the painter.

painter's elevation A sample drawing of each setting detailing painting techniques and colors; provided by the scenic designer.

painter's holiday [*colloq.*] Any oversight or incomplete paint job resulting from the painter's carelessness or negligence.

paint frame A vertical frame to which two-dimensional scenery is attached for upright painting.

perspective Picturing objects on a two-dimensional surface so as to show distance or depth.

plumb line A symmetrically balanced weight attached to string and used to show a perfectly vertical line.

pounce A method whereby a perforated design is transferred to another surface using chalk; the act of pounding chalk dust through a perforated pattern.

pounce bag A cheesecloth bag containing charcoal or indigo chalk dust used for pouncing.

pounce wheel Spiked wheel device that perforates paper.

polyethylene Commercially available clear plastic frequently used by painters as a dropcloth.

primary color A color that cannot be made by combining any other colors; namely, red, yellow, and blue—root of the color wheel.

primer brush Any wide, soft, long-bristled brush used for priming scenery.

primer coat (priming) The initial coat of paint on any new piece of scenery; designed to tighten and seal the weave in the fabric and limit the porosity of wooden surfaces.

puddling A method of texturing whereby two or more colors are dribbled or spattered onto scenery and allowed to run together.

rag rolling Texturing scenery with a rolled rag dipped into a color; technique resembles use of a rolling pin.

rolling The application of color by a paint roller.

scale transfer Proportionally enlarging or reducing a drawing and reproducing it on another surface.

scrim A scenic drop constructed in a wide enough weave so as to allow a transparency to occur under appropriate stage-lighting conditions.

scumble A mottled form of textural painting created by sharply changing the positioning of the brush with the wrist.

secondary color A color resulting from the mixture of two primary colors.

shade A mixture of the base color and black or appropriate dark color; that color used as a lowlight.

shadow wash A transparent dark color used to suggest the shadow of one object cast upon another.

shark's-tooth The most durable form of scrim, providing optimum opacity and transparency.

size Synonomous with glue and "strong size"; thinning will create the working size or size water.

size water Sometimes called "working size," a thinned binder used to size, or shrink, the material on newly covered flats and as the liquefying and binder agent for dry powder pigments.

snap line A retractable string line wound in a chalk-filled container; when stretched over a surface the line is snapped to furnish a perfectly straight chalk line.

spatter Texture by covering a surface with paint droplets.

spatter and drag Dragging spatter droplets with a cloth or push broom in order to produce a linear, grainlike texture.

sponging Achieving texture by applying color with a sponge.

spraying A texturing method using an aerosal, electric, or manual apparatus.

stamping A method of applying designs by pressing shaped sponges or thick carpet patterns against the painting surface.

starch primer A starch solution applied to all new, unpainted drops and scrims that tightens the fabric and retards the bleeding of colors.

stencil(ing) A method of texturing whereby color is applied through holes in a pattern, resulting in a repetitive design on the painting surface.

stencil brush A round-shaped bristle arrangement with a blunt end that is used to push color through stencils in a stippling fashion.

stippling A textural effect produced by pushing the end of a brush or feather duster against the painting surface.

straightedge A notched painting aid that assures the painting of a straight line.

temperature color A color that affects the warmth or coolness of the painting surface.

tint A mixture of the base color and white; that color used as a highlight.

translucent(cy) An element of scenery or a wash through which can be seen a vague and barely discernible image; light may pass through, but not transparent.

transparent(cy) An element of scenery or a wash through which can clearly be seen an underlying image or feature.

value A quality or richness of color.

vanishing point (v.p.) That point on the horizon line at which parallel lines converge, as in perspective drawing.

veining net An arrangement made of twine or muslin used as a tool for flogging, particularly for creating veinings in stonework.

vinyl Compound of plastic derivatives used as a base for scene paint and glazes.

wainscoting Paneling of wood, etc., on the lower sections of walls in a room.

warm Applying to an emotional mood quality derived from the temperature value of color; any exciting, energetic color such as yellow, orange, or red.

wash The thinning of a paint so as to lose its opacity; a dye.

wet blend Two or more colors intermingled when wet on the painting surface.

whiting An inexpensive, nonopaque powder pigment used in priming and to stretch powdered colors.

William Pinnell has designed and painted over one hundred major productions in Canada and the United States and has toured extensively as a performer with the U.S.O. In addition to designing, he has directed several productions that have received critical acclaim at the Edinburgh International Festival Fringe. A graduate of the Hilberry Classic Repertory Company at Wayne State University, Mr. Pinnell is currently an associate professor of drama at the University of Windsor in Ontario, Canada.